NIJ

2 0 0 1

Year in Review

U.S. Department of Justice
Office of Justice Programs

810 Seventh Street, N.W.
Washington, D.C. 20531

John Ashcroft
Attorney General

Deborah J. Daniels
Assistant Attorney General

Sarah V. Hart
Director, National Institute of Justice

This and other publications and products of the U.S. Department of Justice,
Office of Justice Programs, and NIJ can be found on the World Wide Web
at the following sites:

Office of Justice Programs
http://www.ojp.usdoj.gov

National Institute of Justice
http://www.ojp.usdoj.gov/nij

Table of Contents

Introduction

Introduction

In the hours and days after the worst terrorist attacks in U.S. history, workers scrambled through the mountain of rubble from the collapsed towers of the World Trade Center. The determined mission of rescue and the grim task of recovery of victims were well under way, and search teams needed the right tools to perform their tasks safely and effectively. The New York State Emergency Management Office called the National Institute of Justice (NIJ) for onsite assistance. Within 24 hours, a team from NIJ was there to help.

Because of NIJ's investments in counterterrorism research and technology development that have applications to counterterrorism situations [see box on page 3], NIJ was able to establish a temporary office adjacent to the World Trade Center complex to help coordinate technology assistance activities with search and rescue officials. The team called in resources from NIJ's National Law Enforcement and Corrections Technology Center (NLECTC) system to provide immediate assistance to search and rescue efforts. Teams from NLECTC arrived from across the country bringing equipment and technical support.

They brought specialized cameras (canine cameras, pole cameras, and drop cameras), audio equipment, and other search tools and improvised modifications to them onsite. Through a surplus military supply program, NLECTC— Southeast procured $850,000 worth of clothing, boots, ropes, gas masks, helmets, laptop computers, and other equipment for use onsite. NLECTC staff provided engineering, forensic, communications, investigation, and acquisitions support both onsite and offsite.

In the weeks that followed, NIJ rushed to its Web site a draft series of five equipment guides for emergency first responders that had been under development. The guides help agencies make informed decisions on the evaluation and purchase of equipment first responders use during a critical incident. The Web versions of the draft guides have each averaged more than 1,000 hits per month since being posted.

For more information

- See page 17 for a description of the National Law Enforcement and Corrections Technology Center system.

- A complete account of NIJ support of search and recovery efforts at ground zero can be found in the Winter 2002 issue of *Techbeat*, online at http://www.justnet.org/pdffiles/tbwinter2002.pdf.

- Copies of the guides for first responders can be found at http://www.ojp.usdoj.gov/nij/scidocs2001.htm.

Ongoing communication occurs through various means, but the goal is always the same: identify gaps in research knowledge and learn about the needs of criminal justice practitioners.

MISSION OF THE NATIONAL INSTITUTE OF JUSTICE

The National Institute of Justice was created by Congress through the Omnibus Crime Control and Safe Streets Act of 1968, as amended. When it was created 33 years ago, NIJ scientists began a journey to inform policy and practice through research and development about crime and justice. The Institute's mission remains the same today as in 1968—to marry science to criminal justice problem solving and policy development. Specifically, the Omnibus Crime Control and Safe Streets Act of 1968 directs NIJ to:

- Conduct research on the nature and impact of crime and juvenile offending.
- Develop new technologies to reduce crime and improve criminal justice operations.
- Evaluate the effectiveness of criminal justice programs and identify promising new programs.
- Test innovative concepts and model programs in the field.
- Assist policymakers, program partners, and justice agencies.
- Disseminate knowledge to many audiences.

That NIJ was able to respond effectively in the aftermath of the 9-11 attacks is validation of a long-standing commitment to shape its research agenda in response to the needs of the criminal justice field.

NIJ shapes its research agenda and resulting portfolio through ongoing communication with professionals in the field. The communication occurs through various means, but the goal is always the same: identify gaps in research knowledge and learn about the needs of criminal justice practitioners. Collaboration across disciplines helps NIJ shape research strategies that move beyond a strict criminal justice perspective. Partnerships with health, housing, and education researchers and professionals, for example, can result in innovative solutions to criminal justice problems. And NIJ remains flexible enough to shift its research priorities in response to national events, as illustrated in the dramatic aftermath of 9-11.

All of these activities are an important part of NIJ's ongoing efforts to keep its research and communication vehicles relevant to the criminal justice field.

CRITICAL INCIDENT AND COUNTERTERRORISM TECHNOLOGIES

Critical incident and counterterrorism projects at NIJ include:

- **Weapons of mass destruction response.** NIJ is developing technologies to respond to attacks using weapons of mass destruction, including a wearable device that will warn a responder of exposure to chemical and biological hazards.

- **Equipment standards.** NIJ is leading the national effort to establish a comprehensive set of first responder equipment standards.

- **Bomb disposal.** NIJ is evaluating handheld computers for delivering information to bomb technicians, improved x-ray diagnostic systems, bomb robots, and a chemical and biological protective ensemble and is developing a method to neutralize large explosive devices.

- **Border security.** NIJ is supporting an initiative to meet the technology needs of international Integrated Border Enforcement Teams on the Canadian border.

- **Critical incident management.** NIJ began a first-of-its-kind test bed to assess critical incident management technologies that help multiple jurisdictions coordinate their responses. Evaluation of 12 technologies will be completed in 2002.

- **Weapons detection.** Within NIJ's weapons detection portfolio, two technologies in particular show great promise: a walk-through system using magnetometers and a portable device that develops images from body heat in the millimeter wave band of the electromagnetic spectrum. At the Federal Aviation Administration's (FAA's) request, NIJ provided a magnetometer system for that agency to evaluate.

- **Biometrics.** Biometrics are automated methods of recognizing a person based on physiological or behavioral characteristics such as fingerprints, voice patterns, or facial recognition. NIJ is using its considerable investment in biometric development, evaluation, and implementation for public safety agencies in working with the FAA to improve aviation security.

- **Surveillance.** NIJ is developing video surveillance technologies that will alert system operators automatically when a suspect or suspicious activity is detected. These systems can be integrated with weapons detection portals.

NIJ remains flexible enough to shift its research priorities in response to national events, as illustrated in the dramatic aftermath of 9-11.

Highlights of the Year

Research in Action for Communities

Part of NIJ's mission is to test research-based interventions that communities can use to pinpoint the specific nature of their crime problems and develop solutions to those problems.

The highly successful Boston Gun Project, which reduced youth gun violence in Boston, sparked the creation of similar programs in other communities, such as the Strategic Approaches to Community Safety Initiative and the Attorney General's Project Safe Neighborhoods program. These programs are demonstrating that when researchers, practitioners, and policymakers are mobilized in a cooperative effort to solve a targeted problem, solutions begin to appear and problems begin to dissipate.

NIJ's field tests and evaluations find that successful interventions involve comprehensive community-based coalitions, strategic planning, and analysis of research data. Successful community initiatives generally follow five stages of activity:

1. Bringing local leaders and researchers into a committed coalition dedicated to reducing a particular problem.

2. Using a variety of data to identify the specific characteristics of the targeted problem.

3. Designing a strategic intervention based on the data collected.

4. Putting the intervention into place.

5. Assessing the effectiveness of the intervention using data analysis and then adjusting the intervention to improve its effectiveness.

NIJ works with a number of Federal agencies in its efforts to find ways to keep communities safe. In 2001, for example, NIJ and the Bureau of Alcohol, Tobacco, and Firearms (ATF) began demonstrating and evaluating the utility of ATF's Youth Crime Gun Interdiction Initiative, which combines gun tracing data with other law enforcement and local data to identify illegal gun markets in Los Angeles.

Also in 2001, ATF, NIJ, and the Office of Juvenile Justice and Delinquency Prevention cooperated in the release of findings from the evaluation of a gang prevention program called Gang Resistance Education and Training (G.R.E.A.T.). The program showed small but systemic beneficial effects over time. Four years after completing the program, G.R.E.A.T. students reported more negative views about gangs and more favorable attitudes toward the police.

Understanding How Communities Work

Research has shown that ingredients in a winning recipe for community-based problem solving include active partnerships, knowledge-driven decision making, and ongoing strategic assessment. But what are the factors in the neighborhood itself that contribute to successful problem solving?

NIJ's ongoing Project on Human Development in Chicago Neighborhoods, which is conducted in conjunction with the Harvard School of Public Health, is contributing to our understanding of the complex relationship between community, crime, delinquency, family, and individual development.

The project has confirmed that not only do residents' shared mutual trust and expectations make a difference in the level of crime in their neighborhood, but that the nature of bordering neighborhoods also makes a difference.

The findings about the nature of neighborhood residents' trust in one another suggest that efforts to reduce disorder by law enforcement alone—without cooperation from other community entities—may ultimately be short-lived. Any community-based initiative must factor in the extent to which residents have shared social goals and expectations about acceptable levels of disorder.

For more information

■ David M. Kennedy, Anthony A. Braga, Anne M. Piehl, and Elin J. Waring, *Reducing Gun Violence: The Boston Gun Project's Operation Ceasefire*, Research Report, Washington, D.C.: U.S. Department of Justice, National Institute of Justice, October 2001 (NCJ 188741), http://www.ojp.usdoj. gov/nij/pubs-sum/188741.htm. Watch for additional forthcoming titles in the NIJ series *Reducing Gun Violence*, including *Reducing Gun Violence: The St. Louis Consent-to-Search Program; Reducing Gun Violence: Evaluation of the Indianapolis Police Department's Directed Patrol Project;* and

Reducing Gun Violence: Operation Ceasefire in Los Angeles.

■ Robert J. Sampson and Stephen W. Raudenbush, *Disorder in Urban Neighborhoods—Does It Lead to Crime?* Research in Brief, Washington, D.C.: U.S. Department of Justice, National Institute of Justice, February 2001 (NCJ 186049), http://www.ojp.usdoj. gov/nij/pubs-sum/186049.htm.

Tracking Crime in Communities

One of the best tools for uncovering the precise nature of a crime problem is to map it. Crime mapping software and analysis allow neighborhoods to map crime incidents and then overlay other maps that show the location of schools, recreation facilities, bus lines, and other social features to gain a fresh, geographic perspective on how crime and other factors are related.

NIJ supports the crime mapping needs of the criminal justice community through two targeted activities: the Crime Mapping and Analysis Program (CMAP), operated by NLECTC, and the Crime Mapping Research Center (CMRC).

CMAP's mission is to provide technology assistance to State and local agencies in the areas of crime and intelligence analysis and geographic information systems. CMAP has offered more than 35 classes since its inception in 1999, and more than 300 law enforcement personnel have participated. In 2001, CMAP established introductory mapping courses around the Nation, worked with jurisdictions to develop regional crime mapping capabilities, and brought mapping strategies to the corrections community.

NIJ's CMRC continues to focus on research that helps State and local agencies enhance their problem-solving skills. One of NIJ's most active efforts in 2001 was development of a software solution titled the Community Safety Information System, which is helping Memphis, New Haven, and Winston-Salem to map and analyze data that can lead to problemsolving approaches that reduce gun crime.

Also in 2001, staff from NIJ's CMRC worked with the Police Executive Research Forum to develop and publish a primer for mapping criminal activity across jurisdictional boundaries. *Mapping Across Boundaries: Regional Crime Analysis* discusses the real crime-fighting benefits of collaborating across jurisdictions to map crime. The book offers case studies describing how jurisdictions overcame obstacles to sharing databases across their regions.

Making crime mapping information available to the public carries concerns about privacy. Recogniz-

ing potential privacy concerns that could arise when data are shared and made public, NIJ released a report in 2001 that can guide law enforcement personnel, researchers, and others who are creating and sharing crime maps. It contains real-life examples and techniques that, while promoting crime mapping as an effective tool, ensure that concerns about privacy and data confidentiality are met.

For more information

- Julie Wartell and J. Thomas McEwen, *Privacy in the Information Age: A Guide for Sharing Crime Maps and Spatial Data*, Washington, D.C.: U.S. Department of Justice, National Institute of Justice, July 2001 (NCJ 188739), http://www.ojp.usdoj. gov/nij/pubs-sum/188739.htm.

- Nancy G. La Vigne and Julie Wartell, *Mapping Across Boundaries: Regional Crime Analysis*, Washington, D.C.: Police Executive Research Forum, 2001.

Using DNA and Forensic Sciences to Obtain Justice

A large part of NIJ's work revolves around the research, development, and recommendations made by the National Commission on the Future of DNA Evidence. Its recommendations covered issues ranging from how to collect samples at a crime scene to how to test postconviction samples.

From 1997 until its close in 2001, the Commission explored how best to fairly and effectively use

DNA in the criminal justice context. The Commission made a series of recommendations and produced several widely used documents that have influenced both policy and practice.

Reducing the DNA Backlog

DNA technology is advancing rapidly and has become a critical tool for solving crimes. But laboratories cannot keep pace with the

PRODUCTS OF THE NATIONAL COMMISSION ON THE FUTURE OF DNA EVIDENCE

The Future of Forensic DNA Testing: Predictions of the Research and Development Working Group, Issues and Practices, Washington, D.C.: U.S. Department of Justice, National Institute of Justice, November 2000 (NCJ 183697), http://www.ojp.usdoj.gov/nij/pubs-sum/ 183697.htm.

Postconviction DNA Testing: Recommendations for Handling Requests, Issues and Practices, Washington, D.C.: U.S. Department of Justice, National Institute of Justice, September 1999 (NCJ 177626), http://www.ojp. usdoj.gov/nij/pubs-sum/177626.htm.

Understanding DNA Evidence: A Guide for Victim Service Providers, Brochure, Washington, D.C.: U.S. Department of Justice, National Institute of Justice and the Office for Victims of Crime, May 2001, http://www.ojp.usdoj.gov/nij/pubs-sum/BC000657.htm.

Using DNA to Solve Cold Cases: A Guide for Law Enforcement, Research in Practice, Crime Scene Investigation Working Group, Washington, D.C.: U.S. Department of Justice, National Institute of Justice, forthcoming 2002.

What Every Law Enforcement Officer Should Know About DNA Evidence, Brochure, Washington, D.C.: U.S. Department of Justice, National Institute of Justice, September 1999, http://www.ojp.usdoj. gov/nij/pubs-sum/000614.htm.

What Every Law Enforcement Officer Should Know About DNA Evidence, CD-ROM, Washington, D.C.: U.S. Department of Justice, National Institute of Justice, 2000 (NCJ 182992).

What Every Law Enforcement Officer Should Know About DNA Evidence: A Computer Based Training Program, CD-ROM, Washington, D.C.: U.S. Department of Justice, National Institute of Justice, 2000 (NCJ 184479).

collection of DNA samples and the technological advances. Many States have significant backlogs of unanalyzed DNA samples taken from convicted offenders and from crime scenes, including cases where there is no suspect.

In 2001, NIJ awarded approximately $6 million to help 24 States do two things: reduce the number of unanalyzed DNA samples in State databases and reduce the number of cases for which agencies have DNA but no suspect. NIJ's DNA Backlog Reduction Program requires that States analyze a minimum number of cases in which there is no suspect in order to generate matches with the criminal offender database.

Examples of the DNA Backlog Reduction Program's successes:

■ When Virginia analyzed evidence in 366 no-suspect cases, they found that 241 cases produced usable DNA profiles and that 105 of the 241 cases matched to known offenders in either the State or national DNA databases.

■ When Kansas screened 152 no-suspect cases, officials there found that 82 cases had evidence that tested positive for biological fluid and that 54 of the 82 cases yielded a suspect profile that was put into the Criminal Offender Database (CODIS). Those 54 cases produced 15 matches to known offenders.

Since the beginning of the DNA Backlog Reduction Program in fiscal year 2000, more than 347,000 convicted offender samples have been analyzed with Federal funds. The requirement that States analyze no-suspect cases led to analysis of 7,900 of these cases. These efforts generated 824 "hits" or matches—631 matches to known offenders and 193 matches to forensic evidence.

Hundreds of convictions and two exonerations have resulted. But the number of DNA samples needing analysis continues to increase—especially as many States move to collect samples from all convicted felons. For example, when Florida legislators added one more nonviolent offense to the list of offenses for which offenders must give DNA samples, the number of samples taken each year increased by about 40,000.

In August 2001, Attorney General John Ashcroft asked NIJ to pinpoint the issues that continue to impede the full use of DNA, including the reasons for the persistent DNA backlogs. The Attorney General also charged NIJ with finding solutions to those issues.

To meet the Attorney General's request, NIJ assembled a working group of forensic DNA experts representing all areas of criminal justice to consider:

- The nature and extent of DNA backlogs.

- Causes of delays in analyzing DNA.

- Issues surrounding training and certification of laboratory personnel.

- The projected demand for DNA testing.

- The ability to use DNA technology for mass disasters.

- Timetables for implementing new technology.

The working group will analyze these issues thoroughly and broadly for the NIJ Director and recommend ways to address them.

Helping Overburdened Laboratories

In addition to helping laboratories reduce their backlogs, NIJ is helping crime laboratories preserve public confidence and ensure

that forensic evidence is analyzed reliably. Through the Crime Laboratory Improvement Program, NIJ is helping in four crucial areas: analytical services, methods development and evaluation, technology transfer, and training. The Program funds State and local governments to enhance their capability to analyze forensic evidence.

As part of the Crime Laboratory Improvement Program, NIJ created the Forensic Resource Network to give laboratories reliable, permanent access to forensic science technologies, quality assurance systems, and analytical methods. The Network allows State and local crime laboratories to maintain, or obtain, the reliability and sustainability demanded by the field and the public.

The Forensic Resource Network includes the Marshall University Forensic Science Center in Huntington, West Virginia; the National Center for Forensic Science in Orlando, Florida; the National Forensic Science Technology Center in Largo, Florida; and West Virginia University in Morgantown.

These institutions provide State and local laboratories with technology-based training and tools, aid in systems support, and quality assurance products. They also test methods and equipment and evaluate, validate, and distribute information about best practices.

For more information

- Visit the Investigative and Forensic Sciences Division Web site at http://www.ojp.usdoj.gov/nij/ sciencetech/invest.htm.

Improving Law Enforcement

Over the years, research on police interaction with citizens has taken on increased importance, especially as community policing has become a mainstream approach to law enforcement.

Over the years, research on police interaction with citizens has taken on increased importance, especially as community policing has become a mainstream approach to law enforcement. Findings from several projects in 2001 increased our understanding of police-citizen interaction.

Community Interaction With Police

In many communities, residents participate in overseeing local law enforcement agencies. In some, citizen oversight boards investigate allegations of misconduct and recommend actions to the chief or sheriff. Other citizen boards make no recommendations of their own; rather, they review the findings of internal police investigations and endorse or reject the police department's findings.

The various oversight systems have advantages and disadvantages, including monetary costs and benefits. Research suggests that communities must fashion a system that is part of a larger structure of internal and external police accountability and that fits the unique needs of each local situation. The talent, fairness, dedication, and flexibility of key participants are more important to success than is the system's structure.

For more information

■ Peter Finn, *Citizen Review of Police: Approaches and Imple- mentation*, Washington, D.C.: U.S. Department of Justice, National Institute of Justice,

March 2001 (NCJ 184430), http://www.ojp.usdoj.gov/nij/ pubs-sum/184430.htm.

Identifying Problem Officers

A small minority of police officers generates a significant proportion of the citizen complaints that over- sight boards review. An "early warning system," used by a grow- ing number of departments, can help identify problem officers early and intervene through counseling or training to correct problem behavior. Early warning systems are data-based manage- ment tools, most with three basic phases—selection, intervention, and postintervention monitoring. The criteria by which officers are "selected" vary, but may include some threshold combination of citizen complaints, civil litigation, firearms-discharge or use-of-force reports, high-speed pursuits, and resisting-arrest inci- dents. Once officers are selected, interventions designed to change behavior include a combination of counseling, deterrence, education, and training. Postintervention monitoring generally is conducted by the officers' supervisor, but some departments have a more formal process of observation, evaluation, and reporting.

How effective are early warning systems? An NIJ-sponsored inves- tigation of three agencies that use early warning systems found that the systems can reduce citizen complaints and problematic police behavior. Officers in the three departments were involved in fewer citizen complaints and use- of-force incidents after the early warning intervention than before.

But the researchers note that the effectiveness of early warning systems depends upon related policies and procedures that enforce standards of discipline and create a climate of accountability. Early warning systems can be an effective management tool, but should be seen as only one of many tools needed to raise standards of performance and improve the quality of police services.

For more information

■ Samuel Walker, Geoffrey P. Alpert, and Dennis J. Kenney, *Early Warning Systems: Responding to the Problem Police Officer*, Washington, D.C.: U.S. Department of Justice, National Institute of Justice, July 2001 (NCJ 188565), http://www.ojp.usdoj.gov/nij/pubs-sum/188565.htm.

Keeping Officers and Suspects Safe

Apprehension and arrest are interactions that can be quite dangerous for both officers and suspects. NIJ has an extensive portfolio of projects seeking better less-than-lethal tools and techniques to keep both officers and citizens safe during apprehension and arrest. Oleoresin capsicum (OC), or pepper spray, is one. NIJ has funded several projects to increase understanding of the health effects from exposure to OC spray.

One study involved 34 healthy volunteer police cadets. Another looked at suspects who had died in custody and who had been sprayed during their arrest. Both studies suggest that exposure and inhalation do not result in a significant risk for respiratory compromise or asphyxiation.

Although these two studies suggest that pepper spray is safe to use, it is important to note that the studies did not examine the effects of prolonged or long-term exposure to pepper spray.

A third study examined the number of citizen complaints lodged before and after a police department began using OC spray. The research found that citizen complaints of brutality went down after OC spray was introduced. Complaints about excessive force and the number of injured officers also declined. The data sources have some limitations, however. The procedures for identifying officer and suspect injuries differed considerably from agency to agency and within each agency over time. Determination of the number of injuries depended upon the officer's recall of the incident and the degree of detail in his narrative report.

Despite the various limitations of the studies conducted to date, together they are contributing to our knowledge base and clarifying some of the debate about the merits of OC spray as a practical less-than-lethal tool for law enforcement and corrections personnel. NIJ continues to fund research on the health effects of pepper spray used as a less-than-lethal weapon.

For more information

■ Theodore C. Chan, Gary M. Vilke, Jack Clausen, Richard Clark, Paul Schmidt, Thomas Snowden, and Tom Neuman, *Pepper Spray's Effects on a Suspect's Ability to Breathe*, Research in Brief, Washington, D.C.: U.S. Department of Justice, National Institute of

Justice, November 2001 (NCJ 188069), http://www.ojp.usdoj.gov/nij/pubs-sum/188069.htm.

- *The Effectiveness and Safety of Pepper Spray*, Research in Practice, Washington, D.C.: U.S. Department of Justice, National Institute of Justice, forthcoming 2002.

Reducing Law Enforcement and Corrections Officer Stress

Stress is an occupational hazard for law enforcement and corrections officers of all ranks. The effects of stress—low morale, high turnover, absenteeism, and early death—exact a high cost from officers, their families, and their agencies. Since 1996, NIJ has funded efforts to study the nature, extent, and impact of stress on corrections and law enforcement personnel and their families.

In 2001, NIJ launched a six-site field test of a model stress prevention program for law enforcement and corrections personnel and their families. The three corrections and three law enforcement agencies are implementing a model that offers wellness programming, inservice training, supervisor training, and family services.

The model was developed in response to NIJ's previous research, which found that most agency-based programs offer stress-related services only after a critical incident or problem has been identified. The model focuses on preventing stress and developing resiliency in responding to stress. Through the field test, NIJ will collect outcome data to enhance knowledge and ensure that future practice in this area is based on sound research.

Policing on American Indian Reservations

All communities have special needs that law enforcement officers must be sensitive to, but Indian Country offers numerous additional challenges: generally poor economic conditions, unique cultural underpinnings, and vast geographic areas.

A study sponsored by NIJ took a broad look at policing in Indian Country and found that the principles of community policing, which grew out of policing experiences in urban settings, can be effectively applied in Indian Country. In effective community policing, a department must heed the social and cultural norms of the community it serves to gain the trust, respect, and cooperation of the community. The study found that too often this attention to social and cultural norms is lacking among police departments in Indian Country. Many departments operate with little strategic direction from tribal elders and lack methods for communicating directly with their service population. The researchers argue that these problems stem in part from long years of Federal involvement that has resulted in a top-down approach that discourages Indian nations from designing and controlling their own policing institutions.

The research also supported a conclusion reached by others: There is a crisis in policing on Indian reservations characterized by inadequate resources, low morale, poor management, and undue political influence. At the same time, the overall workload of tribal police departments is increasing.

The researchers suggest that tribes and the Federal Government must reconsider the foundations of policing in Indian Country. The challenge, they say, is to create workable, nation-specific policing institutions and approaches informed by traditional customs. Concepts learned from community policing can inform those who face this challenge.

For more information

- Stewart Wakeling, Miriam Jorgensen, Susan Michaelson, and Manley Begay, *Policing on American Indian Reservations,* Research Report, Washington, D.C.: U.S. Department of Justice, National Institute of Justice, September 2001 (NCJ 188095), http://www.ojp.usdoj.gov/nij/ pubs-sum/188095.htm.

Breaking the Drug-Crime Nexus

Some 14 million Americans, or 6.3 percent of all adults, used illicit drugs recently.[1] By contrast, as many as 65 percent of adults who come into the criminal justice system use drugs. Marijuana is the drug of choice in most communities.

Through the Arrestee Drug Abuse Monitoring (ADAM) program, NIJ tracks drug abuse by arrestees and promotes research on substance abuse. In this way, and by evaluating and refining drug detection methods, NIJ is attempting to break the drug-crime nexus.

Drug Use by Arrestees: The ADAM Program

For the past 15 years, NIJ has been conducting interviews and urinalysis among adults and juveniles arrested in selected major urban areas. The findings are more reliable than ever because the samples of the arrestee population are now selected on a more scientifically rigorous basis, and data collection has been standardized

for all the sites. In addition, the recent redesign of the ADAM program added a number of interview questions, including arrestees' participation in drug markets.

All the changes, which required several years of planning and development, were documented and published in 2001.

The international piece of the ADAM program, I-ADAM, was established in 1998 to develop a method that would help researchers begin to compare drug use across countries. Twelve countries are currently affiliated with I-ADAM. Four countries— Australia, England, Malaysia, and the United States—collected data in 2001.

The persistence and gravity of the drug-crime nexus prompted NIJ, in concert with the National Institute on Drug Abuse (NIDA), to update the research agenda the two agencies had developed two decades ago. The updated agenda aims to inform public policy by

---

[1] *Summary of Findings From the 2000 National Household Survey on Drug Abuse,* Washington, D.C.: U.S. Department of Health and Human Services, Substance Abuse and Mental Health Services Administration, Office of Applied Statistics, 2001:1.

highlighting priority topics and "gaps" in knowledge. NIJ and NIDA began developing the agenda in 2000, presented major portions of it at a forum for scholars and policymakers in April 2001, and will publish a report in 2002.

For more information

- Dana Hunt and William Rhodes, *Methodology Guide for ADAM*, Washington, D.C.: U.S. Department of Justice, National Institute of Justice, May 2001, http://www. adam-nij.net.

- Joanna Heliotis, Sarah Kuck, and Dana Hunt, *Analytic Guide for ADAM*, Washington, D.C.: U.S. Department of Justice, National Institute of Justice, May 2001, http://www.adam-nij.net.

- *Toward a Drugs and Crime Research Agenda for the 21st Century*, Washington, D.C.: U.S. Department of Justice, National Institute of Justice, 2002 (NCJ 194616), http://www.ojp.usdoj. gov/nij/pubs-sum/194616.htm.

A New Way to Detect Crack

Among State prisoners, 15 percent said they were using either crack or powder cocaine at the time they committed their offense. In 2001, at least 22 percent of adult male arrestees in 13 of the 28 reporting ADAM sites said they used crack cocaine in the past year, according to preliminary 2001 ADAM data.

Although "self-reports" by arrestees are a valid way to estimate cocaine use, urinalysis is a more objective way. But today's urinalysis technology cannot distinguish between crack and powder. Thanks to NIJ-sponsored research, a solution to this problem may be close at hand.

The key is the discovery of an antibody that identifies crack. The inhaled byproducts of crack, the smokable form of cocaine, appear as "markers" in the urine. The technique for identifying the antibody has been available for several years, but until recently could not be studied using a large sample.

The new procedure, developed by ADAM staff, confirmed what early research had brought to light: Crack use by arrestees is a significant proportion of their cocaine use. When urine samples from arrestees were tested for cocaine, they showed that almost 90 percent of those who tested positive had used crack, not powder. The new procedure also confirmed the tendency to underestimate drug use. The researchers found the proportion of arrestees who used crack was 28 percent, substantially higher than the 15 percent who said they used it.

The procedure is very complex, costly, and in need of refinement, but it appears promising. If crack can be differentiated from powder, it will be possible to measure the relative prevalence of each method of use. NIJ is looking into ways to make the procedure more widely available.

For more information

- K. Jack Riley, Natalie T. Lu, et al., "Monitoring the Crack Epidemic Through Urine Testing: Establishment of Routine Detection Methods," *Addiction Biology* 6 (2001):83–95.

- Natalie T. Lu, Bruce G. Taylor, and K. Jack Riley, "The Validity of Adult Arrestee Self-Reports of Crack Cocaine Use," *American Journal of Drug and Alcohol Abuse* 27(3) (2001):399–419.

Refining Detection Methods

Urinalysis has been the method of choice to detect drug use, but it is invasive and only detects fairly recent use. NIJ is evaluating other methods that might be as effective and efficient while being less invasive.

Testing a sweat patch. The sweat patch is a tamper-proof adhesive pad that absorbs perspiration when applied to the skin. When the patch is removed, drug residues secreted in sweat can be detected. The patch has a longer detection period than urinalysis and thus offers the opportunity for continuous monitoring. It can be worn up to a week, so not as many drug tests are needed and it is less invasive than urinalysis.

But the patch sometimes makes mistakes. It can register drug use when there is none and is more likely than urinalysis to produce false positives, which can occur by contamination of the patch from the surrounding environment or from traces of the drug already on the skin when the patch is applied. NIJ research is working to resolve the contamination and reliability issues.

Testing saliva. Saliva testing is relatively noninvasive, results are rapid, little training is needed to conduct the test, and the kits are portable. They can be used right on the roadside, for example, with people suspected of driving under the influence. Several testing kits are now on the market. NIJ is evaluating four of them to determine their advantages and disadvantages.

For more information

- Melissa Long and David A. Kidwell, *Improving the Pharmcheck™ Sweat Patch: Reducing False Positives From Environmental Contamination and Increasing Drug Detection*, Washington, D.C.: Naval Research Laboratory, December 19, 2001.

Stopping Drug Abuse in Prisons

Inmate drug use in prisons is a continuing problem for corrections administrators. According to a recent study, about 10 percent of drug tests conducted among jail inmates were positive.[2] Many who are incarcerated, along with their accomplices, attempt to smuggle drugs into detention facilities through every conceivable means. Prisons and jails are especially vulnerable to drugs entering the facility through the mail.

In 2001, NIJ began assessing technologies on the market that can rapidly screen mail packages for the presence of drugs. Several types of devices are being tested to find out how accurate they are, how small an amount of a drug they can detect, and whether they can be adapted for use in a correctional facility.

For more information

- Stacy Wright and Robert F. Butler, "Technology Takes On Drug Smugglers: Can Drug Detection Technology Stop Drugs From Entering Prisons?" *Corrections Today* 63(4) (July 2001):66–69.

[2] Doris James Wilson, *Drug Use, Testing, and Treatment in Jails*, Special Report, Washington, D.C.: U.S. Department of Justice, Bureau of Justice Statistics, May 2000 (NCJ 179999), http://www.ojp.usdoj.gov/bjs/pub/pdf/duttj.pdf.

Giving Technology Assistance in the Information Age

By working hand-in-hand with practitioners, NIJ has found ways law enforcement and corrections can take advantage of new technology while mitigating present and potential obstacles.

For most of its existence, NIJ has been helping criminal justice agencies improve their service to the public by developing objective performance standards for equipment. Agencies use these performance standards to make informed decisions about purchasing equipment.

The Information Age offers criminal justice agencies numerous ways to improve service. By working hand-in-hand with practitioners, NIJ has found ways law enforcement and corrections can take advantage of new technology while mitigating present and potential obstacles. Several technology-based efforts are described below.

Enhancing Communications Through Technology

Reliable communications is an essential tool for police officers, firefighters, and emergency medical service personnel in their day-to-day operations. It becomes especially important during critical incidents that involve multiple agencies. A report by the Congressional Research Service found that most jurisdictions lack a unified communications structure that allows personnel from various public safety agencies to communicate directly with one another during an emergency.

Solving the interoperability problem. Interoperability is the ability of two or more public safety agencies to exchange information, when and where it is needed, even when disparate communications or information systems are involved.

For several years, NIJ has been investigating ways to help State and local agencies address the lack of communications interoperability. During 2001, NIJ expanded and enhanced a program called AGILE: Interoperability Strategies for Public Safety.

AGILE aims to improve public safety by developing and evaluating interoperable technology for emergency first responders. Partnerships between NIJ, public safety associations, and industry have been key to the program's success.

One of the first products NIJ evaluated is a system that ties normally incompatible radio systems together. Called the ACU–1000, the technology was tested by the Alexandria (Virginia) Police Department to assess the operational impact and effectiveness of interfacing it with the communications infrastructure of other agencies in the metropolitan Washington, D.C., region.

The evaluation found that agencies could talk to one another via radio equipment that used different frequency bands. They could also communicate via radio using the same frequency band but incompatible modulation formats or trunking techniques. The evaluation of ACU–1000 demonstrated an off-the-shelf interim solution to communications interoperability.

NATIONAL LAW ENFORCEMENT AND CORRECTIONS TECHNOLOGY CENTER

NIJ's commitment to giving technology assistance to State and local criminal justice agencies is demonstrated through NIJ's National Law Enforcement and Corrections Technology Center (NLECTC) system, which serves as an "honest broker" for law enforcement and corrections agencies seeking to implement current and emerging technologies.

The NLECTC system is comprised of five regional centers and complemented by several specialty offices and a national office in Rockville, Maryland.

The regional centers tailor technology solutions by coupling expertise with unique regional characteristics. For example, the newest regional center, in Anchorage, Alaska, gives advice on the most effective equipment to use in cold and blustery climates and ways to minimize training through distance learning.

Other regional centers in the system are the northeast site in Rome, New York; the southeast site in North Charleston, South Carolina; the Rocky Mountain site in Denver, Colorado; and the western site in El Segundo, California.

In 2001, NIJ also expanded the NLECTC specialty centers: The Rural Law Enforcement Technology Center (RULETC) was established in Hazard, Kentucky, to address technology issues unique to historically underserved rural jurisdictions. Although rural jurisdictions make up the majority of law enforcement agencies in the United States, they are on the wrong side of the digital divide when dealing with communications and information technology. RULETC staff are working to bridge that gap through the review of communications problems in Kentucky's rural landscape.

Other specialty centers are the Border Research and Technology Center in San Diego, California; the Office of Law Enforcement Standards in Gaithersburg, Maryland; and the Office of Law Enforcement Technology Commercialization in Wheeling, West Virginia.

NLECTC also assists State and local law enforcement by transferring Federal surplus property to State and local agencies. In 2001, the transfer program moved $135 million worth of property to more than one million sworn officers working in more than 8,000 State and local law enforcement agencies and 500 Federal agencies. In addition, NLECTC staff worked with the Defense Information System Agency to transfer excess computers and equipment worth approximately $1.5 million to law enforcement agencies.

For more information

Visit the NLECTC Web page at http://www.justnet.org.

Solving the shared database problem. Another barrier to effective communication among law enforcement agencies involves sharing databases and mining the data in them. Much of the data that could connect clues and solve crimes is stored in databases that are not compatible or not shared. For example, databases of mug shots may not be able to "talk" to databases that contain information about gang members.

The Tucson (Arizona) Police Department, the University of Arizona's Artificial Intelligence Laboratory, and the National Science Foundation, with support from NIJ, have found a way to pool law enforcement information from various regional and local sources. They created a "smart" database that allows law enforcement to enter disparate clues, search for possible suspects, and thus solve cases more rapidly.

The technology is called Coplink. It gives police and corrections officers a tool that sorts, collates, and relates data so that investigators can search shared databases using key words. For example, officers may know only that a perpetrator's nickname is "Shorty" and that he drives a two-door white car. They can enter these two pieces of information into the database and come up with a number of possible suspects and their addresses. Coplink was tested in 2001 by the Tucson Police Department and is currently being used by the Tucson and Phoenix Police Departments. Expanded use by these and other departments is anticipated in 2002.

For more information

- Visit the AGILE Web page at http://www.agileprogram.org.
- A description of Coplink can be found in the Summer 1999 edition of *Techbeat*, online at http://www.nlectc.org/pdffiles/96242-9.pdf.

Facial Recognition Technologies

New technologies can scan human faces in a real-time setting, then compare the scanned faces to a database of photographs to identify specific individuals. In 2001, NIJ released results from the Facial Recognition Vendor Test, an effort to assess facial recognition systems available for purchase. The test, cosponsored by the Department of Defense Counterdrug Technology Development Program Office and the Defense Advanced Research Projects Agency, provides the counterdrug community and other government agencies with information to use in determining the best use of facial recognition technology in the field.

For more information

- Visit the Counterdrug Technology Development Program Office Facial Recognition Projects Web page at http://www.dodcounterdrug.com/facialrecognition.

Electronic Crime

Electronic crime is an unfortunate byproduct of the Information Age. State and local law enforcement agencies and prosecutorial offices are facing a growing volume of electronic crimes. To help them learn how to better investigate and solve these cases, NIJ is developing a series of reference tools regarding practices and procedures for investigating electronic crime.

The content in the reference tools is guided by practitioners and subject experts who form a working group of professionals from Federal, State, and local criminal justice agencies; and from academic, commercial, and professional organizations. In 2001, NIJ published the first in the series, *Electronic Crime Scene Investigation: A Guide for First Responders*, which provides guidance about handling electronic evidence at crime scenes.

For more information

- *Electronic Crime Scene Investigation: A Guide for First Responders*, Washington, D.C.: U.S. Department of Justice, National Institute of Justice, July 2001 (NCJ 187736), http://www.ojp.usdoj.gov/nij/pubs-sum/187736.htm.

Making Life Safer for Women and Children

Some things we know for sure: violence against women is primarily violence perpetrated by a woman's intimate partner, violence among both men and women is more severe than previously thought,[3] some interventions that work to reduce domestic abuse may not work to prevent elder abuse,[4] and some interventions, like arrest, work for some kinds of perpetrators, but not others.[5] We also know that being abused or neglected as a child increases the likelihood of arrest as a juvenile by 59

[3] Patricia Tjaden and Nancy Thoennes, *Full Report of the Prevalence, Incidence, and Consequences of Violence Against Women: Findings From the National Violence Against Women Survey*, Research Report, Washington, D.C.: U.S. Department of Justice, National Institute of Justice, and the Centers for Disease Control and Prevention, November 2000 (NCJ 183781), http://www.ojp.usdoj.gov/nij/pubs-sum/183781.htm.

[4] Research shows that domestic violence is reduced when a team consisting of a police officer and domestic violence counselor intervenes. When the same strategy was tried in cases involving elders, the victims reported more subsequent abuse. (See Robert C. Davis and Juanjo Medina-Ariza, *Results from an Elder Abuse Prevention Experiment in New York City*, Research in Brief, Washington, D.C.: U.S. Department of Justice, National Institute of Justice, September 2001 (NCJ 188675), http://www.ojp.usdoj.gov/nij/pubs-sum/188675.htm.)

[5] Christopher D. Maxwell, Joel H. Garner, and Jeffrey A. Fagan, *The Effects of Arrest on Intimate Partner Violence: New Evidence From the Spouse Assault Replication Program*, Research in Brief, Washington, D.C.: U.S. Department of Justice, National Institute of Justice, July 2001 (NCJ 188199), http://www.ojp.usdoj.gov/nij/pubs-sum/188199.htm.

percent, as an adult by 28 percent, and for a violent crime by 30 percent.[6]

Over the years, NIJ has conducted much research and evaluated many programs in an effort to find ways to reduce the violence perpetrated against women and their children. But in many cases, building knowledge about what works has been slow because it is impossible to devise experiments that isolate the many complex factors that make up human relationships.

How Health Care Providers Can Help Victims

Well-documented medical records can make domestic violence court cases stronger.

Many health care protocols and training programs recognize the importance of documenting abuse. But medical records often contain shortcomings that prevent the prosecutor from using them as evidence in court. The shortcomings may be as mundane as indecipherable handwriting or as key as missing photographs of injuries.

With funds transferred from the Violence Against Women Office within the Office of Justice Programs, NIJ supported researchers who examined the medical charts of almost 100 domestic violence victims. The resulting analysis produced a set of suggestions for ways health care providers can improve the admissibility of evidence.

Suggestions include:

- Documenting factual information rather than making summary statements.
- Photographing the injuries.
- Noting the patient's demeanor.
- Clearly indicating the patient's statements as his or her own.
- Avoiding terms that imply doubt about the patient's reliability.
- Refraining from using legal terms.
- Writing legibly.

A followup study is developing a protocol for improving the way domestic violence is documented by the medical profession. Training for practitioners is a key part of this followup study.

For more information

- Nancy E. Issacs and V. Pualani Enos, *Documenting Domestic Violence: How Health Care Providers Can Help Victims*, Research in Brief, Washington, D.C.: U.S. Department of Justice, National Institute of Justice, October 2001 (NCJ 188564), http://www.ojp.usdoj.gov/nij/pubs-sum/188564.htm.

An Update on the "Cycle of Violence"

Childhood victimization represents a widespread, serious social problem. Previous research shows childhood physical and sexual abuse leads to delinquency,

---

[6] Cathy S. Widom and Michael G. Maxfield, *An Update on the "Cycle of Violence,"* Research in Brief, Washington, D.C.: U.S. Department of Justice, National Institute of Justice, March 2001 (NCJ 184894), http://www.ojp.usdoj.gov/nij/pubs-sum/184894.htm.

and onset of maltreatment may increase the variety, seriousness, and duration of problems. And violence begets violence—today's abused children too often become tomorrow's violent offenders.

In 2001, NIJ released the updated results of a longitudinal study that compared the arrest records of abused and/or neglected children with arrest records for children who were not abused or mal-treated, and findings reinforced the phenomena known as the "cycle of violence."

Being abused or neglected as a child greatly increases the likelihood of that child later being arrested. Maltreated children were younger at the time of their first arrest, committed nearly twice as many offenses, and were arrested more frequently than youth and adults who were not maltreated as children. Physically abused and neglected (versus sexually abused) children were the most likely to be arrested later for a violent crime. In contrast to earlier research findings, the new results indicate that abused and neglected females were also at increased risk of arrest for violence as juve-niles and adults. Researchers cite three implications for juvenile authorities and child welfare professionals: intervene early, recognize that neglect can be as high risk as physical abuse in contributing to future violent behavior, and reexamine out-of-home placement policies.

For more information

- Cathy S. Widom and Michael G. Maxfield, *An Update on the "Cycle of Violence,"* Research in Brief, Washington, D.C.: U.S. Department of Justice, National

Institute of Justice, March 2001 (NCJ 184894), http://www. ojp.usdoj.gov/nij/pubs-sum/ 184894.htm.

Evaluating Services for Victims

State-based criminal justice agen-cies receive funds to strengthen their response to violence against women. The funding comes from the Violence Against Women Office; the program is called STOP (Services, Training, Officers, and Prosecutors). NIJ evaluates the effectiveness of the programs funded with STOP grants.

An evaluation of 6 years of STOP programs suggested that, overall, the awards have been a successful way to improve criminal justice services to women. The evaluators found that collaboration among service providers is key to success and suggested that State STOP agencies make local coordination a priority.

The evaluation found that more programs for victims of sexual assault were needed and recom-mended that greater focus be placed on funding such programs. The evaluation also recommended that agencies and States put into place better data and evaluation systems so that the impact of STOP programs can be better measured.

For more information

- Martha R. Burt, Janine M. Zweig, Cynthia Andrews, Asheley Van Ness, Neal Parikh, Brenda K. Uekert, and Adele V. Harrell, *2001 Report: Evaluation of the STOP Formula Grants to Combat Violence Against Women,* Washington, D.C.: Urban Institute, September 2001.

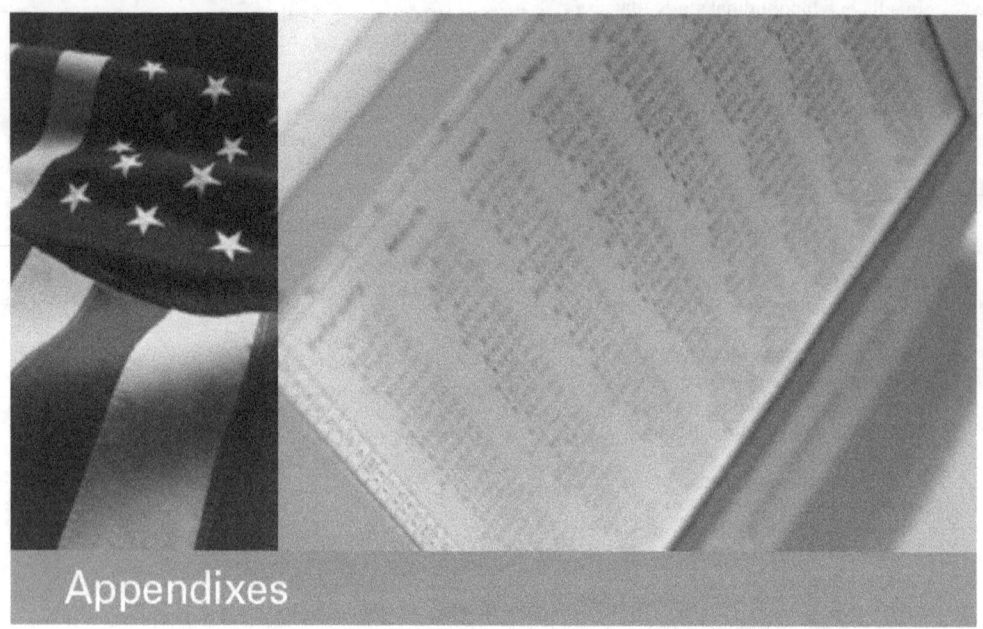

Appendixes

APPENDIX A

Organization

NIJ's internal organization, shown in exhibit 1, "Organization of NIJ," reflects the discrete missions of each component of the Institute:

- The Office of the Director sets the Institute's agenda, develops strategic plans and policies, initiates collaboration with other government and private agencies, and oversees the Institute's budget and management activities.

- The Office of Development and Communications develops and tests research-based programs, brings promising new practices to the attention of the field, and communicates findings and technological innovations through multiple methods. Priority is given to the needs of State and local officials and criminal justice practitioners. The International Center focuses on crime and justice issues that transcend national boundaries and have impact on State and local criminal justice systems.

- The Office of Research and Evaluation develops, conducts, directs, and supervises comprehensive research and evaluation activities. The range of research and

evaluation cuts across a wide array of distinct topics within the Institute's charter. Three programs operate as distinct centers of activity: the Arrestee Drug Abuse Monitoring (ADAM) program; the Crime Mapping Research Center; and the Data Resources Program, which ensures the preservation and availability of research and evaluation data collected through NIJ-funded research.

- The Office of Science and Technology directs and supervises technology research, development, and demonstrations to provide law enforcement and corrections agencies access to the best technologies available. It also provides technology assistance so that these agencies can enhance their capabilities to improve efficiency and effectiveness. Technology assistance is provided through the network of the regional National Law Enforcement and Corrections Technology Center.

EXHIBIT 1: ORGANIZATION OF NIJ

As of June 1, 2002

National Institute of Justice
Sarah V. Hart, Director
Glenn R. Schmitt, Deputy Director

Office of the Director

Office of Development and Communications
Michael Dalich, Director

- The International Center
James O. Finckenauer, Director

- Development Division
A. Elizabeth Griffith, Director

- Communications Division
Gerald P. Soucy, Director

Office of Research and Evaluation
Thomas E. Feucht, Acting Director

- Justice Systems Research Division
Christopher Innes, Director

- Violence and Victimization Research Division
Margaret A. Zahn, Director

- Drugs and Crime Research Division
Henry Brownstein, Director

- Crime Control and Prevention Research Division
Winifred L. Reed, Acting Director

Office of Science and Technology
David G. Boyd, Director

- Research and Technology Development Division
A. Trent DePersia, Director

- Technology Support Division
Sharla Rausch, Director

- Technology Assistance Division
Marc Caplan, Director

- Investigative and Forensic Science Division
Lisa Forman, Director

APPENDIX B
Financial Data

EXHIBIT 2: TRENDS IN NIJ'S RESEARCH AND DEVELOPMENT PORTFOLIO,
FY 1994–2001

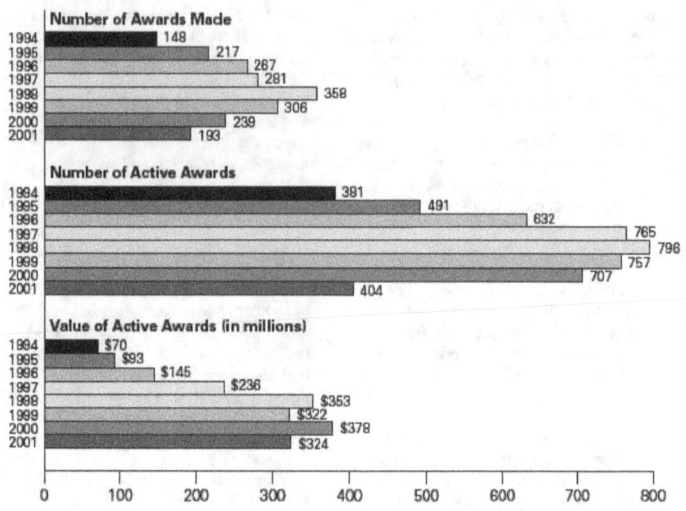

EXHIBIT 3: SOURCES OF NIJ FUNDS, IN MILLIONS, FY 1994–2001

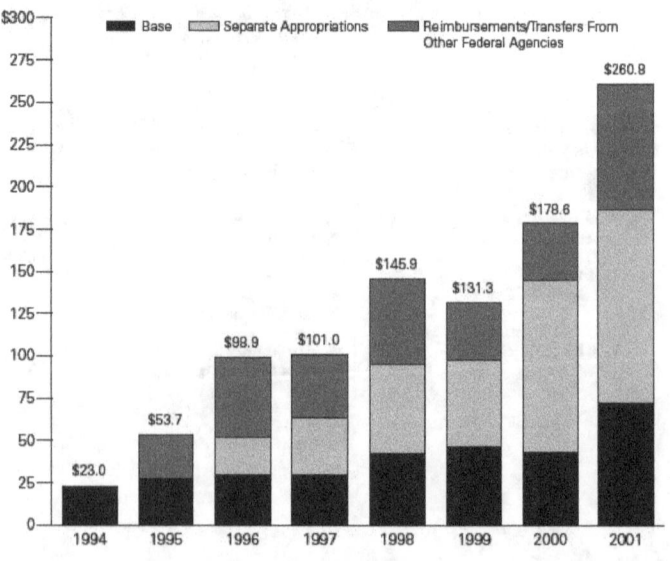

EXHIBIT 4: ALLOCATION OF NIJ FUNDS AS A PERCENTAGE OF
TOTAL EXPENDITURES,* FY 2001

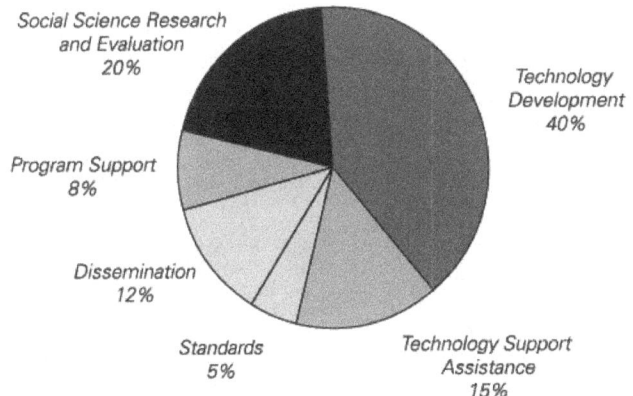

*Total expenditures of $260.8 million includes NIJ's base
appropriation of $69.8 million plus separate appropriations
and funds transferred from other agencies.

25

APPENDIX C

Awards Made in Fiscal Year 2001

(includes first-time awards and supplements to previous awards)

COMMUNITY JUSTICE

Community Mapping, Planning, and Analysis of Safety Strategies—City of Redlands East Valley Initiative
Redlands Police Department
James R. Bueermann
$624,199   01–MU–MU–K012

Community Mapping, Planning, and Analysis for Safety Strategies—Milwaukee
Milwaukee, City of
Jim Pingel
$625,000   01–IJ–CX–K005

University of Wisconsin–Milwaukee
Peter Maier
$275,000   01–MU–MU–K015

Development of Crime Forecasting and Mapping Systems for Use by Police
Carnegie Mellon University
Thomas Eagan
$233,500   01–IJ–CX–0018

Development and Implementation of a Crime Mapping Training Lab
National Corrections and Law Enforcement Training and Technology Center
G. Steve Morrison
$96,545   01–LT–BX–K007

CORRECTIONS

Electronic Supervision Tools: Improving Practice and Technology
Council of State Governments/American Probation and Parole Association
Carl Wicklund
$99,720   99–LT–VX–K001

Offender Prediction and Classification
University of Texas–Austin
William R. Kelly
$15,000   01–IJ–CX–0003

Prevalence and Management of Infectious Disease Conditions in the Correctional Setting
University of Texas Health Science Center–San Antonio
Jacques Baillargeon
$254,701   01–IJ–CX–0023

Tale of Two Laws Revisited: Investigating the Impact of Prisoner Litigation Reform
National Center for State Courts–Virginia
Fred Cheesman
$135,644   01–IJ–CX–0013

Technology in Corrections
American Correctional Association
John Greene
$174,663   96–LB–VX–K004

Tenth National Survey of HIV/AIDS, STD's, and TB in Corrections
Abt Associates Inc.
Theodore Hammett
$202,414   01–IJ–CX–K018

Understanding the Female Offender
University of New Mexico
Lisa Broidy
$195,655   01–IJ–CX–0034

Validating a Brief Jail Mental Health Screen
University of Maryland–Baltimore
Jack E. Scott
$281,412   01–IJ–CX–0030

COURTS

Reentry Courts Process Evaluation
Research Triangle Institute
Pamela Lattimore
$50,000   01–DD–BX–0071

CRIME PREVENTION

Crime Prevention, General
Breaking the Cycle Research Demonstration
Pierce County Alliance
Terree Schmidt
$300,000   98–IJ–CX–K011

Exploration of the Correlates of Specialization and Escalation
Arizona State University
Todd Armstrong
$30,814   01–IJ–CX–0004

Program on Human Development in Chicago Neighborhoods/Program on Human Development and Criminal Behavior
Harvard College
Felton J. Earls
$2,200,000   93–IJ–CX–K005

Strategic Approaches to Community Safety Initiative (SACSI)
SACSI Research Partnership
Michigan State University
Timothy S. Bynum
$229,915   01–IJ–CX–K006

Strategic Approaches to Community Safety Initiative
Reed Institute
Stefan J. Kapsch
$25,000   99–IJ–CX–0025

Strategic Approaches to Community Safety Initiative
Rochester Institute of Technology
John Klofas
$229,947   01–IJ–CX–K009

Strategic Approaches to Community Safety Initiative
University of New Mexico
Albert Harper
$229,993   01–IJ–CX–K001

INFORMATION DISSEMINATION AND REVIEW OF CRIMINAL JUSTICE RESEARCH

Annual Review of Justice Research
Castine Research Corporation
Michael Tonry
$202,446   92–IJ–CX–K044

Applying Fuzzy Statistical Methods to Survey Data
Sam Houston State University
Steven Jay Cuvelier
$35,000   01–IJ–CX–0002

Campbell Crime and Justice Group
University of Pennsylvania
Lawrence Sherman
$34,994   01–IJ–CX–0032

Center for Criminal Justice Technology
Mitretek Systems, Inc.
Steven L. Pomerantz
$997,796   01–LT–BX–K002

Committee on Law and Justice Core Support
National Academy of Sciences
Judith P. Cohn
$280,000   01–MU–MU–0007

Crime and Justice Atlas: Centennial Edition
Justice Research and Statistics Association
Joan C. Weiss
$37,000   00–IJ–CX–0005

Journal of Criminology and Public Policy
John Jay College–Research Foundation of the City University of New York
Todd Clear
$113,961   00–IJ–CX–0036

Technology Conference Support
Center for Technology Commercialization, Inc.
James Scutt
$1,072,855   99–LT–VX–K021

INTERNATIONAL CRIME

The Internet Studio: Building the Infrastructure for the World Justice Information Network
Rule of Law Foundation
Sergey Chapkey
$107,970   98–IJ–CX–K004

NIJ Rule-of-Law Transition Support Activities
Abt Associates Inc.
Terence Dunworth
$674,200   01–IJ–CX–K002

Preventing Corruption and Crime in the Republic of Georgia: A Three-Pronged Cultural Approach
National Strategy Information Center, Inc.
Roy Godson
$222,500   01–IJ–CX–K016

Trafficking in Persons in the United States
Croft Institute for International Studies
Kevin B. Bales
$199,395   01–IJ–CX–0027

INVESTIGATIVE AND FORENSIC SCIENCES

Forensics, General
Central Piedmont Community College Forensic Institute
Central Piedmont Community College
Michael Horn
$498,900   01–RC–CX–K009

Direct In-Situ ID of Inks to Expedite Forensic Analysis
Iowa State University
John McClelland
$160,000   01–LT–BX–K004

DNA: Lessons From the Past, Problems for the Future
Brooklyn Law School
Margaret Berger
$31,235   01–LT–BX–0002

Forensic Equipment for Southern Regional Crime Laboratory
Arizona Department of Public Safety
Todd A. Griffith
$698,460   01–RC–CX–K007

Forensic ID Training and Research Resources at West Virginia University
West Virginia University Research Corporation
Edwin Rood
$3,000,000   01–RC–CX–K003

Forensic Science and Crime Scene Technology Conference
Frenzy Expo, LLC
Elia Beeken
$100,000   01–LT–BX–0001

Marshall University Forensic Science Center
Marshall University
Ron Schelling
$502,382   01–RC–CX–K002

National Center for Forensic Science
University of Central Florida
Terri Vallery
$2,489,477   98–IJ–CX–K003

Neurobiological and Psychosocial Correlates and Predictors
University of Mississippi Medical Center
Angelos Halaris
$1,000,000   01–IJ–CX–0036

Pattern Recognition Techniques in Investigative and Forensic Sciences
Institute for Linguistic Evidence, Inc.
Carole E. Chaski
$84,000   98–LB–VX–0065

Perfluorocarbon Detection Experiment—II
Tracer Detection Technology Corporation
Jay Fraser
$99,780   01–LT–BX–K005

Procurement of Fingerprint Examination Instruments
Kansas Bureau of Investigation
Mike VanStratton
$149,670   01–RC–CX–K012

Service Quality in Crime Laboratories
National Forensic Science Technology Center
William J. Tilstone
$2,594,280   00–RC–CX–K001

Support to the 15th Meeting of the International Association of Forensic Sciences
International Association of Forensic Sciences, Inc.
Barry A.J. Fisher
$15,062   98–LB–VX–0011

Time-Sensitive Investigations: Arnold Markle Symposium 2001
University of New Haven–School of Public Safety
Albert Harper
$27,750   01–LT–BX–K001

DNA 5-Year Plan
Development of Rapid, Immobilized Probe Assay for the Detection of mtDNA Variation
Children's Hospital–Oakland Research Institute
Kathleen Gonzalez
$259,080   96–IJ–CX–0028

Microdevice for Automated, Ultra-High-Speed, and Portable DNA Forensics
Whitehead Institute for Biomedical Research
Daniel J. Ehrlich
$1,102,790   98–LB–VX–K022

DNA Laboratory Improvement Program
Automated STR Mixture Analysis
Cybergenetics Co.
Mark Perlin
$396,525   01–IJ–CX–K003

Charge Tags as Electronic Labels for DNA Microchip Testing
Carnegie Mellon University
Victor W. Weedn
$180,849   01–IJ–CX–K012

Development of Y SNP Assays for a Multicolor Fluorescence Detection System
American University
Janice Idyll
$55,568   01–IJ–CX–K013

Homogenous Fluorescent PCR Assays for Forensically Informative Sites Over the Entire mtDNA Genome
American Registry of Pathology
Thomas J. Parsons
$465,082   00–IJ–CX–K010

LINE Elements: New Source of Genomic Variation-DNA Profiling
Louisiana State University and Agricultural and Mechanical College
Mark Batzer
$370,513   01–IJ–CX–K004

Locus-Specific Brackets and Multiplex PCR for Y Chromosome STR's
Oligotrail, LLC
Debang Liu
$224,588   01–IJ–CX–K008

Plant DNA Typing by AFLP
University of New Haven–School of
Public Safety
Albert Harper
$259,868   01–IJ–CX–K011

Renovation and Expansion of
SEMO Regional Crime Lab
Southeast Missouri State University
Robert C. Briner
$750,000   01–MU–MU–K004

Replacement and Enhancement of
Lab Instrumentation and Equipment
Vermont Department of Public Safety
Eric Buel
$498,900   01–RC–CX–K005

CODIS Backlog Reduction
DNA Backlog Reduction Program
Bode Technology Group, Inc.
Thomas J. Bode
$2,297,252   01–RC–CX–K010

DNA Backlog Reduction Program
Fairfax Identity Laboratories
Daniel B. Demers
$103,392   01–RC–CX–K011

DNA Backlog Reduction Program
GeneScreen
John Rader
$90,400   01–RC–CX–K008

DNA Backlog Reduction Program
Georgia Bureau of Investigation
George Herrin, Jr.
$482,710   01–RC–CX–0003

DNA Backlog Reduction Program
Lifecodes Corporation
Bruce Boeko
$22,932   01–RC–CX–0002

DNA Backlog Reduction Program
Myraid Genetic Laboratories, Inc.
Brian E. Ward
$2,746,764   01–RC–CX–K014

DNA Backlog Reduction Program
North Carolina Department of Justice
Mark S. Nelson
$146,400   01–RC–CX–0001

DNA Backlog Reduction Program
ReliaGene Technologies, Inc.
Sudhir K. Sinha
$60,200   01–RC–CX–K013

Equipment Replacement and DNA Remodel
Alaska Department of Public Safety
George M. Taft, Jr.
$1,249,926   01–RC–CX–K001

Georgia Crime Lab Improvement and
Case Backlog Reduction Project
Georgia Bureau of Investigation
Terry Mills III
$648,570   01–RC–CX–K006

Laboratory Information Management
System Implementation
Ohio Bureau of Criminal Identification
and Investigation
Roger Kahn
$498,898   01–RC–CX–K004

Less-Than-Lethal Incapacitation
Less-Than-Lethal Equipment Review
National Security Research, Inc.
Jeffrey Schwartz
$24,752   01–LT–BX–K009

Less-Than-Lethal Technology Support
Pennsylvania State University
Andrew F. Mazzara
$77,464   01–RD–CX–K002

Ring Airfoil Projectile System for Less-
Than-Lethal Application
Guilford Engineering Associates, Inc.
David Findlay
$80,990   97–IJ–CX–K019

Communication and Information
Technologies
Advanced Generation Interoperability
for Law Enforcement
University of Denver–Colorado Seminary
Robert Epper
$712,015   01–RD–CX–K001

Capital Wireless Integrated Network
University of Maryland–College Park
George Ake
$373,666   01–RB–CX–K001

Distributed COPLINK Database and
Concept Space Development
Tucson, City of
Jennifer Schroeder
$395,077   00–RB–CX–K001

Establish and Publish a Suite of Very
Narrow Band Voice and Data Standards
Association of Public Safety Communica-
tions Officials International, Inc.
Craig M. Jorgensen
$100,000   97–LB–VX–K002

Indiana Hoosier Safe-T
Indiana State Police
Lester Miller
$2,993,400   01–LT–BX–K003

**Interoperable Communications
for Public Safety Agencies**
Sheriffs' Association of Texas
Steve Westbrook
$168,169   01–MU–MU–K017

**Law Enforcement Data Mining Analytical
Tools Developed in Support of the
Washington/Baltimore HITDA**
University of Maryland–College Park
Thomas H. Carr
$1,470,000   99–LT–VX–K010

**National Communications Interoperability
Assessment**
Johns Hopkins University–Applied Physics
Laboratory
Darcy Brudin
$49,730   00–MU–MU–K007

**Spatial Knowledge Mining and
Information Sharing**
University of Virginia
Donald E. Brown
$210,000   00–RB–CX–K004

**Statewide LAWNET Communications
Project**
New Hampshire Department of Safety
Frederick H. Booth
$3,900,201   01–MU–MU–K010

Training and Simulation Technologies
**Rural Law Enforcement Technology
Support**
Eastern Kentucky University
Pam Collins
$250,000   00–MU–MU–K008

Technology Outreach Program
Primedia Workplace Learning
Josh Klarin
$236,956   00–MU–MU–K020

Critical Incident Response/
Counterterrorism Technologies
**Incident Command Management System
Test Bed**
Camber Corporation
Ed Wolcoff
$250,000   01–MU–MU–K014

Program Assessment, Policy,
and Coordination
Criminology and Public Policy
American Society of Criminology
Chris Eskridge
$206,356   01–IJ–CX–0015

Public Safety Technology Partnership
Center for Technology Commercialization, Inc.
Lisa Hecker
$248,931   01–LT–BX–K011

Risk Assessment Validation Study
Johns Hopkins University
Jacquelyn Campbell
$523,669   00–WT–VX–0011

**SEASKATE Technology and Policy
Assessment Executive Panel**
SEASKATE, Inc.
E.A. Burkhalter, Jr.
$598,630   01–MU–MU–K003

Surplus Property Program
Ultimate Enterprises Limited
Michael Simpson
$245,458   96–LB–VX–K002

**Technology and Policy Assessment
Liability Task Group**
SEASKATE, Inc.
E.A. Burkhalter, Jr.
$278,431   01–MU–MU–K001

Technology Assistance, National Law
Enforcement and Corrections Technology
Center (NLECTC)
**Governance and Technology Delivery
Processes for NLECTC**
Elberton, City of
Ruth M. Davis
$378,446   98–LB–VX–0001

NLECTC—Rocky Mountain Region
University of Denver–Colorado Seminary
Robert Epper
$1,775,508   96–MU–MU–K012

**NLECTC—Rural Law Enforcement
Technology Center**
Eastern Kentucky University
Pam Collins
$1,457,000   01–MU–MU–K009

NLECTC—Southeast Region
South Carolina Research Authority
Gary Mastrandrea
$5,028,402   97–MU–MU–K020

**NLECTC Supplemental Funding for
Development of OLES Web Site**
Aspen Systems Corporation
Richard S. Rosenthal
$2,789,914   96–MU–MU–K011

NLECTC—West
Aerospace Corporation
Jay Glowacki
$1,728,190   00–MU–MU–K004

Operation of the Office of Law Enforcement
Technology Commercialization
Wheeling Jesuit University
Carole Coleman
$2,800,000   98–IJ–CX–K002

LAW ENFORCEMENT

Policing, General
**Assessing Police Officers' Decision
Making and Discretion**
University of South Carolina
Geoffrey Alpert
$247,877   01–IJ–CX–0035

**An Assessment of Indian Country Law
Enforcement in PL–280 States**
University of California–Los Angeles
Carole Goldberg
$299,993   01–IJ–CX–0031

**The Cop Crunch: Identifying Strategies for
Dealing Effectively With the Recruiting and
Hiring Crisis in Law Enforcement**
Police Executive Research Forum
Lorie Fridell
$210,995   01–IJ–CX–0024

**Does the Way Police Treat Citizens in
Routine Encounters Shape Community
Opinion of the Police?**
Vera Institute of Justice, Inc.
Robert C. Davis
$106,509   01–IJ–CX–0038

**Examining Minority Trust and
Confidence in the Police**
University of Illinois
Darnell F. Hawkins
$343,132   01–IJ–CX–0021

**Exploring the Reasons for Public
Trust and Confidence**
New York University
Tom Tyler
$196,488   01–IJ–CX–0029

**Rethinking Minority Attitudes
Toward the Police**
George Washington University
Helen Spencer
$202,273   01–IJ–CX–0016

**Transferring Responsibility for Child
Welfare to a Law Enforcement Agency:
An Evaluation**
University of Pennsylvania
Richard Gelles
$194,762   00–IJ–CX–0002

**Why Do Corporations Obey Environmental
Law?**
University of Maryland–College Park
Sally Simpson
$315,792   01–IJ–CX–0020

Community Policing
**Blueprint for Sustaining Community-
Based Initiatives**
Winston-Salem State University
Sylvia Oberle
$49,070   01–IJ–CX–0025

**Criminal Careers of Places:
A Longitudinal Study**
University of Maryland–College Park
David Weisburd
$286,967   01–IJ–CX–0022

Corrections and Law Enforcement
Family Support (CLEFS)
CLEFS Law Enforcement Field Test
Knoxville, City of
Cheri Matlock
$100,000   01–FS–BX–K004

Correction Officer Stress Management
New Jersey Department of Corrections
Therese Matthews
$99,239   01–LT–BX–K013

Law Enforcement and Family Stress
Duluth, City of
Peg Johnson
$94,046   01–FS–BX–K002

**North Miami Beach Police "SOS"
(Stop Our Stress)**
North Miami Beach, City of
Mike Gordon
$60,300   01–FS–BX K003

Staff and Family Support Program
Iowa Department of Corrections
Larry Brimeyer
$100,000   01–LT–BX–K012

**Wisconsin Youth Counselor Stress
Reduction Program**
Wisconsin Department of Corrections
Shelly Hagan
$100,000   01–FS–BX–K001

SCHOOLS

Berkeley High School Security Project
Berkeley Unified School District
Frank Lynch
$305,265   01–LT–BX–K008

Increasing the Utility of School Incident Data
Abt Associates Inc.
Thomas Rich
$201,785   01–IJ–CX–0026

Integration of Law Enforcement Into School Safety
Milwaukee Public Schools
Peter Pochowski
$280,000   01–IJ–CX–0037

Role of Law Enforcement in Public School Safety
University of Cincinnati
Lawrence F. Travis III
$405,262   01–IJ–CX–0011

Safe School Technologies
MATCOM
William Walsh
$49,566   99–LT–VX–K015

Safe Schools, Law Enforcement, and Corrections Research Support
George Mason University
Stephen D. Mastrofski
$49,890   00–RD–CX–K003

Software Radio for School Safety
Vanu, Inc.
Andrew D. Beard
$149,750   01–RD–CX–K003

Testing a Drug Detection and Identification System in Secondary Schools Using Nontoxic Aerosol Technology
Mistral Security, Inc.
Eyal Banai
$356,925   00–RD–CX–K004

SENTENCING

Impact of Truth-in-Sentencing on Length of Stay in Prison
Urban Institute
Avinash Bhati
$14,067   98–CE–VX–0006

Maryland Department of Juvenile Justice Partnership to Study Waiver Effects
University of Baltimore
Cindy Smith
$145,972   98–CE–VX–0018

TECHNOLOGY DEVELOPMENT

Officer Protection and Crime Prevention Technologies
Activity-Suppressing Light Barrier
Johns Hopkins University–Applied Physics Laboratory
Maurice Permodo
$75,034   01–LT–BX–K006

Applying Behavioral Economics and Game Theory to the Problems of Optimal Crime Control
University of California–Los Angeles
Mark Kleiman
$145,000   01–IJ–CX–0033

Biometric Authentication System
Integrated Technology Solutions, Inc.
James L. Gossard
$235,000   01–RB–CX–K002

Consolidated Advanced Technologies for Law Enforcement
University of New Hampshire
W. Thomas Miller III
$3,492,300   01–LT–BX–K010

Development of a Smart Gun Prototype Using Handgrip Recognition
Jeffrey Moser
$299,510   01–IJ–CX–K010

Enhancing Imputation Methodologies for County-Level UCR Data
University of Illinois
Michael D. Maltz
$34,997   01–IJ–CX–0006

Face Recognition and Intelligent Software Development
Analytic Services, Inc.
Antonio R. Harris
$1,787,021   98–LB–VX–K021

Improved Thermal Control Body Armor
Johns Hopkins University–Applied Physics Laboratory
Darcy Brudin
$199,560   01–RD–CX–K004

Law Enforcement Technology Dissemination
Eastern Kentucky University
Tom Thurman
$230,424   99–DT–CX–K001

Law Enforcement Technology Dissemination and Training
Eastern Kentucky University
James T. Thurman
$46,742   99–LT–VX–K002

Multiband Antenna System for AGILE
Mission Research Corporation
Hirsch Chizever
$105,936   00–RB–CX–K002

Secure Weapons System
FN Manufacturing, Inc.
Jeffrey R. Rankin
$1,271,826   01–IJ–CX–K017

Southwest Border States Anti-Drug
Information System
Criminal Information Sharing Alliance
Glen Gillum
$8,773,400   97–LB–VX–K009

Technology Information Exchange for
State and Local Law Enforcement
International Association of Chiefs of Police
John Firman
$174,102   99–LT–VX–K004

VICTIMIZATION AND
VICTIM SERVICES

Victim Services, General
**National Impact Evaluation of
Victim Service Programs**
Urban Institute
Martha Burt
$161,163   99–WT–VX–0010

**Victim Rights and Services for
the Pueblo of Laguna**
New Mexico State University
Joan Crowley
$90,000   01–VI–GX–0011

Elder Abuse
Bruising in the Geriatric Population
University of California–Irvine
Laura Mosqueda
$110,745   01–IJ–CX–K014

**Identifying Forensic Markers
in Elder Sexual Abuse**
Boston College
Stephen Erickson
$99,264   01–IJ–CX–K015

**Recommendations for Elder Abuse
and Related Forensic Issues**
American Bar Association
Lori Stiegel
$100,000   01–IJ–CX–K007

VIOLENCE

Violence, General
**Explaining Males' and Females'
Delinquency**
University of Nebraska–Omaha
Finn Esbensen
$15,000   01–IJ–CX–0009

**Gender, Economic Transformation,
and Urban Violence**
University of Florida–Gainesville
Karen F. Parker
$32,440   01–IJ–CX–0008

Impact of Immigration in Ethnic-
Specific Violence in Miami
Florida International University
Ramiro Martinez, Jr.
$61,997   01–IJ–CX–0012

Violence Against Women
and Family Violence
**Context, Motives, and Meaning
of Partner Violence**
University of North Texas
Linda L. Marshall
$499,960   01–WT–BX–0504

**Culturally Focused Batterer Counseling
for African-American Men**
Indiana University of Pennsylvania
Edward Gondolf
$356,321   01–WT–BX–0003

**Development and Validation of a Coercive
Control Measure**
Cosmos Corporation
Mary Ann Dutton
$430,924   01–WT–BX–0503

**Ecological Model of Battered Women's
Experience Over Time**
Georgetown University
Mary Ann Dutton
$569,586   01–WT–BX–0001

**Empirical Examination of a Theory of
Women's Use of Violence in Intimate
Relationships**
Yale University
Susanne Swan
$388,803   01–WT–BX–0502

**Evaluation of a Multisite Demonstration
of Collaborations to Address Domestic
Violence and Child Maltreatment**
Caliber Associates
Sharon Bishop
$749,518   00–MU–MU–0014

**Evaluation of a Multisite Demonstration
for Enhanced Judicial Oversight of
Domestic Violence Cases**
Urban Institute
Adele Harrell
$640,000   99–WT–VX–K005

**Explaining the Prevalence, Context,
and Consequences of Dual Arrest in
Intimate Partner Cases**
University of Massachusetts–Lowell
Research Foundation
David Hirschel
$428,189   01–WT–BX–0501

**Female-on-Female Assault
in an Urban Area**
Rutgers State University–New Jersey
Nancy M. Hirschinger
$15,000   01–WT–BX–0505

**Impact of Intimate Partner Violence
on Women's Labor Force**
University of Illinois
Stephanie Riger
$299,407   01–WT–BX–0002

**National Sexual Violence Prevention
Conference**
Illinois Coalition Against Sexual Assault
Polly Poskin
$75,000   01–WT–BX–0004

**Testing the Impact of Court Monitoring
and Batterer Intervention Program**
New York, City of
Michele Sviridoff
$294,129   01–WT–BX–0506

**When Silenced Voices Speak: Exploratory
Study of Prostitute Homicide Cases**
MCP Hahnemann University
Jonathan A. Dudek
$15,000   01–IJ–CX–0001

Firearms
**Ballistics Matching Using 3D Images
of Bullets and Cartridge Cases**
Intelligent Automation, Inc.
Benjamin Bachrach
$54,982   97–LB–VX–0008

**Gun Policy, Gun Violence, and
America's Cities**
Brookings Institution
Bruce Katz
$35,000   01–IJ–CX–0010

Improving Research and Data on Firearms
National Academy of Sciences
Carol Petrie
$175,613   00–IJ–CX–0034

New Haven Gun Project
Spectrum Associates Market Research, Inc.
Eliot Hartstone
$42,000   99–IJ–CX–K001

Strategic Disruption of Firearms Markets
Rand Corporation
Jack Riley
$399,993   01–IJ–CX–0028

YOUTH

**Assessment of the Special Programming
and Management Needs of Youths**
University of Texas–Austin
Yvonne Murray
$193,289   01–IJ–CX–0014

**Between Two Worlds: Prosecuting
Adolescents in Juvenile Court**
New York University
Aaron Kupchik
$14,942   01–IJ–CX–0005

Breaking-the-Cycle Project for Juveniles
Lane County Department of Youth Services
Stephen Carmichael
$7,444   99–IJ–CX–K017

**Breaking-the-Cycle Project for Juveniles
Evaluation**
Research Triangle Institute
Pamela Lattimore
$300,000   99–IJ–CX–0032

**Evaluation of Juvenile Justice Mental
Health Initiative With Randomized Design**
University of Missouri–St. Louis
G. David Curry
$200,000   01–IJ–CX–0017

**Impact of Juvenile Justice Involvement
on Educational Outcomes**
Northwestern University
Paul Hirschfield
$15,000   01–IJ–CX–0007

**Police Problem-Solving Strategies
for Dealing With Youth- and Gang-
Related Firearms**
Rand Corporation
Peter Greenwood
$65,000   98–IJ–CX–0043

APPENDIX D

Materials Published in Fiscal Year 2001

Most NIJ materials are free and can be obtained from these three sources:

1. NIJ: http://www.ojp.usdoj.gov/nij.

2. National Criminal Justice Reference Service (NCJRS): http://www.ncjrs.org, 800–851–3420, P.O. Box 6000, Rockville, MD 20849–6000.

3. (For science and technology materials) National Law Enforcement and Corrections Technology Center (NLECTC): http://www.justnet.org, 800–248–2742.

ADAM REPORTS

ADAM Preliminary 2000 Findings on Drug Use and Drug Markets—Adult Male Arrestees, Taylor, Bruce G., Nora Fitzgerald, Dana Hunt, Judy A. Reardon, and Henry H. Brownstein, Research Report, December 2001, 36 pages, NCJ 189101.

Analytic Guide for ADAM, Heliotis, Joanna, Sarah Kuck, and Dana Hunt, May 2001, 51 pages.

Methodology Guide for ADAM, Hunt, Dana, and William Rhodes, May 2001, 82 pages.

2000 Annualized Site Reports, Research Report, June 2001, 400 pages, NCJ 192943.

CORRECTIONS

Addressing Correctional Officer Stress: Programs and Strategies, Finn, Peter, Issues and Practices, February 2001, 129 pages, NCJ 183474.

A National Study Comparing the Environments of Boot Camps With Traditional Facilities for Juvenile Offenders, MacKenzie, Doris Layton, Angela R. Gover, and Gaylene Styve, Research in Brief, August 2001, 19 pages, NCJ 187680.

A Resource Guide to Law Enforcement, Corrections, and Forensic Technologies, Office of Justice Programs and Office of Community Oriented Policing Services, Resource Guide, May 2001, 103 pages, NCJ 186822.

What Future for "Public Safety" and "Restorative Justice" in Community Corrections? Smith, Michael E., Research in Brief, June 2001, 19 pages, NCJ 187773.

COURTS

Documenting Domestic Violence: How Health Care Providers Can Help Victims, Isaac, Nancy E., and V. Pualani Enos, Research in Brief, October 2001, 10 pages, NCJ 188564.

Pretrial Services Programs: Responsibilities and Potential, Mahoney, Barry, Bruce D. Beaudin, John A. Carver III, Daniel B. Ryan, and Richard B. Hoffman, Issues and Practices, March 2001, 130 pages, NCJ 181939.

A Resource Guide to Law Enforcement, Corrections, and Forensic Technologies, Office of Justice Programs and Office of Community Oriented Policing Services, Resource Guide, May 2001, 103 pages, NCJ 186822.

Sentencing Guidelines: Reflections on the Future, Lubitz, Robin L., and Thomas W. Ross, Research in Brief, June 2001, 15 pages, NCJ 186480.

CRIME PREVENTION

Crime Mapping and Analysis by Community Organizations in Hartford, Connecticut, Rich, Thomas, Research in Brief, March 2001, 19 pages, NCJ 185333.

Disorder in Urban Neighborhoods—Does It Lead to Crime? Sampson, Robert J., and Stephen W. Raudenbush, Research in Brief, February 2001, 13 pages, NCJ 186049.

Pretrial Services Programs: Responsibilities and Potential, Mahoney, Barry, Bruce D. Beaudin, John A. Carver III, Daniel B. Ryan, and Richard B. Hoffman, Issues and Practices, March 2001, 130 pages, NCJ 181939.

Reducing Gun Violence: The Boston Gun Project's Operation Ceasefire, Kennedy, David M., Anthony A. Braga, Anne M. Piehl, and Elin J. Waring, Research Report, October 2001, 60 pages, NCJ 188741.

Results From an Elder Abuse Prevention Experiment in New York City, Davis, Robert C., and Juanjo Medina-Ariza, Research in Brief, September 2001, 12 pages, NCJ 188675.

An Update on the "Cycle of Violence," Widom, Cathy S., and Michael G. Maxfield, Research in Brief, March 2001, 14 pages, NCJ 184894.

DRUGS AND CRIME

ADAM Preliminary 2000 Findings on Drug Use and Drug Markets: Adult Male Arrestees, Taylor, Bruce G., Nora Fitzgerald, Dana Hunt, Judy A. Reardon, and Henry H. Brownstein, Research Report, December 2001, 36 pages, NCJ 189101.

Breaking the Juvenile Drug-Crime Cycle, Vander Waal, Curtis J., Duane C. McBride, Yvonne M. Terry-McElrath, and Holly VanBuren, Research Report, May 2001, 24 pages, NCJ 186156.

Perspectives on Crime and Justice: 1999–2000 Lecture Series, Volume 4, Zimring, Franklin, Richard B. Freeman, William A. Vega, Lawrence W. Sherman, and Heather B. Weiss, Research Forum, March 2001, 135 pages, NCJ 184245.

The Rise of Marijuana as the Drug of Choice Among Youthful Adult Arrestees, Golub, Andrew, and Bruce D. Johnson, Research in Brief, June 2001, 26 pages, NCJ 187490.

Trace Detection of Narcotics Using a Pre-concentrator/Ion Mobility Spectrometer System, Parmeter, John E., and Gary A. Eiceman, Law Enforcement and Corrections Standards and Testing Program, April 2001, 15 pages, NCJ 187111.

INTERNATIONAL

Crime, Criminal Justice, and Criminology in Post-Soviet Ukraine, Foglesong, Todd S., and Peter H. Solomon, Jr., Research Report, July 2001, 119 pages, NCJ 186166.

Democratizing the Police Abroad: What to Do and How to Do It, Bayley, David H., Research Report, June 2001, 108 pages, NCJ 188742.

The Threat of Russian Organized Crime, Finckenauer, James O., and Yuri A. Voronin, Research Report, June 2001, 35 pages, NCJ 187085.

INVESTIGATIVE SCIENCES

Biometrics Catalog online, July 2001.

Development of NIST Standard Bullets and Casings Status Report, Song, J., and T.V. Vorburger, Law Enforcement and Corrections Standards and Testing Program, November 2000, 15 pages, NCJ 184434.

Electronic Crime Scene Investigation: A Guide for First Responders, National Institute of Justice, NIJ Guide, July 2001, 98 pages, NCJ 187736.

Flammable and Combustible Liquid Spill/Burn Patterns, Putorti, Jr., Anthony D., Jay A. McElroy, and Daniel Madrzykowski, Law Enforcement and Corrections Standards and Testing Program, March 2001, 18 pages, NCJ 186634.

Improved Analysis of DNA Short Tandem Repeats With Time-of-Flight Mass Spectrometry, Butler, John M., and Christopher H. Becker, Science and Technology Research Report, October 2001, 54 pages, NCJ 188292.

Understanding DNA Evidence: A Guide for Victim Service Providers, National Institute of Justice and Office for Victims of Crime, Brochure, May 2001, 8 pages, BC 000657.

LAW ENFORCEMENT

Antenna System Guide, NIJ Guide 202–00, Kissick, W.A., W.J. Ingram, J.M. Vanderau, and R.D. Jennings, April 2001, 61 pages, NCJ 185030.

Citizen Review of Police: Approaches and Implementation, Finn, Peter, Issues and Practices, March 2001, 209 pages, NCJ 184430.

Community Prosecution in Washington, D.C., Boland, Barbara, Research Report, June 2001, 46 pages, NCJ 186274.

Crime Mapping and Analysis by Community Organizations in Hartford, Connecticut, Rich, Thomas, Research in Brief, March 2001, 19 pages, NCJ 185333.

Development of NIST Standard Bullets and Casings Status Report, Song, J., and T.V. Vorburger, Law Enforcement and Corrections Standards and Testing Program, November 2000, 15 pages, NCJ 184434.

Early Warning Systems: Responding to the Problem Police Officer, Walker, Samuel, Geoffrey P. Alpert, and Dennis J. Kenney, Research in Brief, July 2001, 17 pages, NCJ 188565.

Electronic Crime Needs Assessment for State and Local Law Enforcement, Stambaugh, Hollis, David S. Beaupre, David J. Icove, Richard Baker, Wayne Cassaday, and Wayne P. Williams, Research Report, March 2001, 77 pages, NCJ 186276.

Electronic Crime Scene Investigation: A Guide for First Responders, NIJ Guide, July 2001, 98 pages, NCJ 187736.

Flammable and Combustible Liquid Spill/Burn Patterns, Putorti, Jr., Anthony D., Jay A. McElroy, and Daniel Madrzykowski, Law Enforcement and Corrections Standards and Testing Program, March 2001, 18 pages, NCJ 186634.

Guide for the Selection of Chemical Agent and Toxic Industrial Material Detection Equipment for Emergency First Responders, NIJ Guide 100–00, Volume I, June 2000, 70 pages, NCJ 184449.

Guide for the Selection of Chemical Agent and Toxic Industrial Material Detection Equipment for Emergency First Responders, NIJ Guide 100–00, Volume II, June 2000, 452 pages, NCJ 184450.

An Introduction to Biological Agent Detection Equipment for Emergency First Responders, NIJ Guide 101–00, December 2001, 46 pages, NCJ 190747.

The New Structure of Policing: Description, Conceptualization, and Research Agenda, Bayley, David H., and Clifford D. Shearing, Research Report, July 2001, 60 pages, NCJ 187083.

Pepper Spray's Effects on a Suspect's Ability to Breathe, Chan, Theodore C., Gary M. Vilke, Jack Clausen, Richard Clark, Paul Schmidt, Thomas Snowden, and Tom Neuman, Research in Brief, November 2001, 13 pages, NCJ 188069.

Privacy in the Information Age: A Guide for Sharing Crime Maps and Spatial Data, Wartell, Julie, and J. Thomas McEwen, Research Report, July 2001, 66 pages, NCJ 188739.

Reducing Gun Violence: The Boston Gun Project's Operation Ceasefire, Kennedy, David M., Anthony A. Braga, Anne M. Piehl, and Elin J. Waring, Research Report, October 2001, 60 pages, NCJ 188741.

A Resource Guide to Law Enforcement, Corrections, and Forensic Technologies, Office of Justice Programs and Office of Community Oriented Policing Services, Resource Guide, May 2001, 103 pages, NCJ 186822.

Selection and Application Guide to Personal Body Armor, November 2001, 121 pages, NCJ 189633.

Trace Detection of Narcotics Using a Preconcentrator/Ion Mobility Spectrometer System, Parmeter, John E., and Gary A. Eiceman, Law Enforcement and Corrections Standards and Testing Program, April 2001, 15 pages, NCJ 187111.

Users' Guide for Hand-Held and Walk-Through Metal Detectors, Paulter, Nicholas G., Law Enforcement and Corrections Standards and Testing Program, January 2001, 56 pages, NCJ 184433.

RESEARCH AND EVALUATION

Breaking the Juvenile Drug-Crime Cycle, Vander Waal, Curtis J., Duane C. McBride, Yvonne M. Terry-McElrath, and Holly VanBuren, Research Report, May 2001, 24 pages, NCJ 186156.

Citizen Review of Police: Approaches and Implementation, Finn, Peter, Issues and Practices, March 2001, 209 pages, NCJ 184430.

Crime, Criminal Justice, and Criminology in Post-Soviet Ukraine, Foglesong, Todd S., and Peter H. Solomon, Jr., Research Report, July 2001, 113 pages, NCJ 186166.

Democratizing the Police Abroad: What to Do and How to Do It, Bayley, David H., Research Report, June 2001, 108 pages, NCJ 188742.

Development of NIST Standard Bullets and Casings Status Report, Song, J., and T.V. Vorburger, Law Enforcement and Corrections Standards and Testing Program, November 2000, 15 pages, NCJ 184434.

Disorder in Urban Neighborhoods—Does It Lead to Crime? Sampson, Robert J., and Stephen W. Raudenbush, Research in Brief, February 2001, 13 pages, NCJ 186049.

Early Warning Systems: Responding to the Problem Police Officer, Walker, Samuel, Geoffrey P. Alpert, and Dennis J. Kenney, Research in Brief, July 2001, 17 pages, NCJ 188565.

The Effects of Arrest on Intimate Partner Violence: New Evidence From the Spouse Assault Replication Program, Maxwell, Christopher D., Joel H. Garner, and Jeffrey A. Fagan, Research in Brief, July 2001, 22 pages, NCJ 188199.

Guide to the Technologies of Concealed Weapon and Contraband Imaging and Detection, NIJ Guide 602–00, Paulter, Nicholas G., February 2001, 66 pages, NCJ 184432.

1999 Survey of Forensic Reference Materials, National Institute of Standards and Technology, March 2001, 98 pages, NCJ 187237.

Pepper Spray's Effects on a Suspect's Ability to Breathe, Chan, Theodore C., Gary M. Vilke, Jack Clausen, Richard Clark, Paul Schmidt, Thomas Snowden, and Tom Neuman, Research in Brief, November 2001, 13 pages, NCJ 188069.

Perspectives on Crime and Justice: 1999–2000 Lecture Series, Volume 4, Zimring, Franklin, Richard B. Freeman, William A. Vega, Lawrence W. Sherman, and Heather B. Weiss, Research Forum, March 2001, 135 pages, NCJ 184245.

Policing on American Indian Reservations, Wakeling, Stewart, Miriam Jorgensen, Susan Michaelson, and Manley Begay, Research Report, Revised September 2001, 115 pages, NCJ 188095.

Privacy in the Information Age: A Guide for Sharing Crime Maps and Spatial Data, Wartell, Julie, and J. Thomas McEwen, Research Report, July 2001, 66 pages, NCJ 188739.

Reducing Gun Violence: The Boston Gun Project's Operation Ceasefire, Kennedy, David M., Anthony A. Braga, Anne M. Piehl, and Elin J. Waring, Research Report, October 2001, 60 pages, NCJ 188741.

Results From an Elder Abuse Prevention Experiment in New York City, Davis, Robert C., and Juanjo Medina-Ariza, Research in Brief, September 2001, 12 pages, NCJ 188675.

The Rise of Marijuana as the Drug of Choice Among Youthful Adult Arrestees, Golub, Andrew, and Bruce D. Johnson, Research in Brief, June 2001, 26 pages, NCJ 187490.

Sentencing Guidelines: Reflections on the Future, Lubitz, Robin L., and Thomas W. Ross, Research in Brief, June 2001, 15 pages, NCJ 186480.

The Threat of Russian Organized Crime, Finckenauer, James O., and Yuri A. Voronin, Research Report, June 2001, 35 pages, NCJ 187085.

SCIENCE AND TECHNOLOGY

Antenna System Guide, NIJ Guide 202–00, Kissick, W.A., W.J. Ingram, J.M. Vanderau, and R.D. Jennings, April 2001, 61 pages, NCJ 185030.

Biometrics Catalog online, July 2001.

Development of NIST Standard Bullets and Casings Status Report, Song, J., and T.V. Vorburger, Law Enforcement and Corrections Standards and Testing Program, November 2000, 15 pages, NCJ 184434.

Electronic Crime Needs Assessment for State and Local Law Enforcement, Stambaugh, Hollis, David S. Beaupre, David J. Icove, Richard Baker, Wayne Cassaday, and Wayne P. Williams, Research Report, March 2001, 77 pages, NCJ 186276.

Electronic Crime Scene Investigation: A Guide for First Responders, National Institute of Justice, NIJ Guide, July 2001, 98 pages, NCJ 187736.

Flammable and Combustible Liquid Spill/Burn Patterns, Putorti, Jr., Anthony D., Jay A. McElroy, and Daniel Madrzykowski, Law Enforcement and Corrections Standards and Testing Program, March 2001, 18 pages, NCJ 186634.

Guide for the Selection of Chemical and Biological Decontamination Equipment for Emergency First Responders, NIJ Guide 103–00, Volume I, National Institute of Justice, October 2001, 98 pages, NCJ 189724.

Guide for the Selection of Chemical and Biological Decontamination Equipment for Emergency First Responders, NIJ Guide 103–00, Volume II, National Institute of Justice, October 2001, 186 pages, NCJ 189725.

Guide to the Technologies of Concealed Weapon and Contraband Imaging and Detection, NIJ Guide 602–00, Paulter, Nicholas G., February 2001, 66 pages, NCJ 184432.

Improved Analysis of DNA Short Tandem Repeats With Time-of-Flight Mass Spectrometry, Butler, John M., and Christopher H. Becker, Science and Technology Research Report, October 2001, 54 pages, NCJ 188292.

An Introduction to Biological Agent Detection Equipment for Emergency First Responders, NIJ Guide 101–00, National Institute of Justice, December 2001, 46 pages, NCJ 190747.

1999 Survey of Forensic Reference Materials, National Institute of Standards and Technology, March 2001, 98 pages, NCJ 187237.

Pepper Spray's Effects on a Suspect's Ability to Breathe, Chan, Theodore C., Gary M. Vilke, Jack Clausen, Richard Clark, Paul Schmidt, Thomas Snowden, and Tom Neuman, Research in Brief, November 2001, 13 pages, NCJ 188069.

Privacy in the Information Age: A Guide for Sharing Crime Maps and Spatial Data, Wartell, Julie, and J. Thomas McEwen, Research Report, July 2001, 66 pages, NCJ 188739.

Trace Detection of Narcotics Using a Pre-concentrator/Ion Mobility Spectrometer System, Parmeter, John E., and Gary A. Eiceman, Law Enforcement and Corrections Standards and Testing Program, April 2001, 15 pages, NCJ 187111.

Understanding DNA Evidence: A Guide for Victim Service Providers, National Institute of Justice and Office for Victims of Crime, Brochure, May 2001, 8 pages, BC 000657.

Users' Guide for Hand-Held and Walk-Through Metal Detectors, Paulter, Nicholas G., Law Enforcement and Corrections Standards and Testing Program, January 2001, 56 pages, NCJ 184433.

VICTIMS

Documenting Domestic Violence: How Health Care Providers Can Help Victims, Isaac, Nancy E., and V. Pualani Enos, Research in Brief, October 2001, 10 pages, NCJ 188564.

The Effects of Arrest on Intimate Partner Violence: New Evidence From the Spouse Assault Replication Program, Maxwell, Christopher D., Joel H. Garner, and Jeffrey A. Fagan, Research in Brief, July 2001, 22 pages, NCJ 188199.

Results From an Elder Abuse Prevention Experiment in New York City, Davis, Robert C., and Juanjo Medina-Ariza, Research in Brief, September 2001, 12 pages, NCJ 188675.

Understanding DNA Evidence: A Guide for Victim Service Providers, National Institute of Justice and Office for Victims of Crime, Brochure, May 2001, 8 pages, BC 000657.

An Update on the "Cycle of Violence," Widom, Cathy S., and Michael G. Maxfield, Research in Brief, March 2001, 14 pages, NCJ 184894.

OTHER

Crime and Justice, A Review of Research (volume 28), published by the University of Chicago Press, Journals Division, with support from NIJ.

Perspectives on Crime and Justice: 1999–2000 Lecture Series, Volume 4, Zimring, Franklin, Richard B. Freeman, William A. Vega, Lawrence W. Sherman, and Heather B. Weiss, Research Forum, March 2001, 135 pages, NCJ 184245.

NIJ JOURNAL

October 2000, Cover Story: "Getting to Know Neighborhoods," by G. Thomas Kingsley and Kathryn L.S. Pettit, 40 pages, JR 000245.

January 2001, Cover Story: "Policing on American Indian Reservations," by Stewart Wakeling, Miriam Jorgensen, and Susan Michaelson, 40 pages, JR 000246.

April 2001, Cover Story: "Challenging the Russian Mafia Mystique," by James O. Finckenauer and Elin Waring, 28 pages, JR 000247.

SOLICITATIONS FOR RESEARCH AND EVALUATION

Application for FRENZY Conference and Expo Support, January 2001.

Communications Interoperability and Information Sharing Technologies (AGILE R&D) Solicitation, June 2001, 14 pages.

COMPASS: Research Partner for Milwaukee COMPASS, Request for Proposals, March 2001.

Context and Consequences of Mutual Intimate Partner Violence, March 2001, 10 pages, SL 000474.

Corrections and Law Enforcement Family Support, Solicitation for the Implementation of the Law Enforcement and Corrections Field Tests—Corrections Field Tests, January 2001.

Corrections and Law Enforcement Family Support, Solicitation for the Implementation of the Law Enforcement and Corrections Field Tests—Law Enforcement Field Tests, January 2001.

Crime and Justice Research and Evaluation: American Indian and Alaska Native Issues, January 2001, 14 pages, SL 000455.

Data Resources Program: Funding for the Analysis of Existing Data, August 2000, 10 pages, SL 000437.

Examining Minority Trust and Confidence in the Police, November 2000, 9 pages, SL 000448.

Graduate Research Fellowship Program: Tomorrow's Research Community, 4 pages, NCJ 172869.

NIJ School Safety Web-Based Curriculum Solicitation, June 2001, 10 pages.

NIJ "Smart Gun" Solicitation, June 2001, 13 pages.

Office of Research and Evaluation 2001 Solicitation for Investigator-Initiated Research, September 2000, 13 pages, SL 000442.

Request for Applications for Reentry Courts Process Evaluation, January 2001, 21 pages.

Solicitation for Convicted Offender DNA Backlog Reduction Program (FY 2001), March 2001, 22 pages, SL 000472.

Solicitation for a Demonstration/Evaluation of the Utility of ATF's Youth Crime Gun Interdiction Initiative, March 2001, 13 pages, SL 000473.

Solicitation for Forensic DNA Research and Development, FY 2001, February 2001, 10 pages, SL 000461.

Solicitation for General Forensic Research and Development for FY 2001, June 2001, 12 pages.

Solicitation for a Research Partner for the East Valley, California, COMPASS Initiative, April 2001.

Trafficking in Persons in the U.S., June 2001, 10 pages.

W.E.B. DuBois Fellowship Program: NIJ Residential Research Opportunity, November 2000, 12 pages, SL 000450.

NIJ ANNUAL REPORT

2000 Annual Report to Congress, August 2001, 50 pages, NCJ 189105.

CATALOGS OF PUBLICATIONS

NCJRS Catalog #55, November/December 2000, 20 pages, BC 000279.

NCJRS Catalog #56, January/February 2001, 20 pages, BC 000280.

NCJRS Catalog #57, March/April 2001, 20 pages, BC 000281.

NCJRS Catalog #58, May/June 2001, 24 pages, BC 000282.

NCJRS Catalog #59, July/August 2001, 20 pages, BC 000283.

NCJRS Catalog #60, September/October 2001, 20 pages, BC 000284.

APPENDIX E

Key Conferences

Annual Conference on Criminal Justice Research and Evaluation, "Enhancing Policy and Practice," July 22–25, 2001, Washington, D.C. In 2001, NIJ's primary annual conference focused on how research can help shape policy and practice. Attendance topped 900.

Fifth Annual International Crime Mapping Conference, "Translating Spatial Research Into Practice," December 1–4, 2001, Dallas, Texas. The 2001 conference featured 500 participants representing more than a dozen countries.

Fifth Annual Mock Prison Riot, April 29– May 3, 2001, Moundsville, West Virginia. This annual event, which takes place in a former maximum security correctional facility, is designed to demonstrate correc-

tions technologies through realistic simulations. The 2001 event included 1,350 attendees representing 35 States and 7 countries; 77 technologies were showcased.

Fourth National Workshop on Sentencing and Corrections Challenges, May 31–June 1, 2001, Jacksonville, Florida. More than 200 attendees from 42 States attended this workshop. Topics included DNA issues in sentencing and corrections, offender reentry, juvenile offenders, restorative justice, sex offender management, and the reinvention of probation and parole.

National Conference on Science and the Law, October 4–6, 2001, Miami, Florida. Designed to explore the role of science and scientists in the criminal justice system. Nearly 200 attended.

The National Institute of Justice is the
research, development, and evaluation
agency of the U.S. Department of Justice
and is solely dedicated to researching crime
control and justice issues. NIJ provides
objective, independent, nonpartisan,
evidence-based knowledge and tools to
meet the challenges of crime and justice,
particularly at the State and local levels.

The National Institute of Justice is a
component of the Office of Justice
Programs, which also includes the
Bureau of Justice Assistance, the
Bureau of Justice Statistics, the Office
of Juvenile Justice and Delinquency
Prevention, and the Office for
Victims of Crime.

*Photo Sources: GettyImages and
PictureQuest.*

NCJ 195075

www.ingramcontent.com/pod-product-compliance
Lightning Source LLC
Chambersburg PA
CBHW070505290526
45790CB00003B/1110

9 781502 794574